For Ann-Marie,

a welcome !

MW00889279

The Bite of History

Patriarchy Messing with Me and Food for 85 Years

AN AUTOBIOGRAPHY BY

CAROLINE ANAYA

Nutrition Scientist &
Fitness Professional

Copyright © 2018 Caroline Anaya

All rights reserved.

ISBN- 13: 978-1986732758

ISBN- 10:1986732754

The Bite of History

TABLE OF CONTENTS

I have been able to see my life as from a great altitude, as a sort of landscape, and with a deepening sense of the connection of all its parts.

The River of Consciousness
Final Essays of Oliver Sacks

ACKNOWLEDGMENTS

I am grateful for the many friends who helped me pull this book together with suggestions and ideas. Janet Elder reminisced with me about our shared single-parent experiences in Florida. I appreciate the guidance of Jo Ann Lordahl, a kindred spirit and seasoned writer. Photo editing was by Bonita Dewiliby-Moore. Designs by Shoi designed the book cover and gave the interior a professional touch. Lisa Gatlin edited the final draft and Gina Edwards of Around the Writer's Table provided a final review before publication. JoAnne Talamo provided ongoing moral support and formatted the book for publication.

Valerie Manno Giroux, PhD, Department of Communication Studies, University of Miami encouraged me: "It's your book. Write it how you want."

DISCLAIMER

Some names and identifying details in this book have been changed to protect the privacy of the people involved.

The Bite of History

Patriarchy Messing with Me and Food for 85 Years

INTRODUCTION

Life was relatively simple back in the '30s. While the country was in the midst of The Great Depression, our small town, mile-high Flagstaff, Arizona, managed reasonably well. Families were stable. Dads went to work, women managed the home, and kids had chores. Food came from local farms, gardens, and the dairy. We just cooked it, ate it, and were healthy.

My "woman training" started at birth. As a toddler, I was sweeping and dusting. By the age of three, I learned to keep my body parts private. By four, I could wash and iron. At five, I was keeping secrets. At six, I started helping Mom in the kitchen. The magic of making food into a meal that we ate and that kept us healthy set the seeds for my life-long passion: Foods and Nutrition.

Once I began school, Dad made it clear I was to be an 'A' student. Mom's advice was "Be curious. Question everything. Trust your instincts." I saw my future: a loving wife, talented homemaker, compassionate parent and excelling in a glorious career.

I take you through those years with tales that young people nowadays will find hard to imagine. There was community, sharing, instinctive kindness; the environment was clean and quiet. Only a few folks had home phones; there were no personal phones or cameras, no library, no global awareness, no TV, no internet, no fast food, and rarely meds. By 21, we were on our own.

A well-beaten path led straight through high school and college into a career.

In college, I blossomed from a geeky girl into a committed woman. I studied hard, building the foundation for a career. I was well rewarded with positions as a research chemist: with the Human Nutrition Research Branch of the United States Department of Agriculture (USDA), next, with the US Fish & Wildlife Service, and on to a fascinating stint with industry at the Food and Flavor Labs of Arthur D. Little, Inc. I was on fire! Doing the research, supervising research, publishing, and giving talks about my work, even at the United Nations Children's Fund (UNICEF).

But then I made a mistake.

I was oblivious to the cultural undercurrent that tripped me up. I didn't know that I was ignorant about everything woman: bodies, Kotex, sex, marriage. Silence from the adults; hearsay from other girls; awkward encounters. Lots of mistakes. I had no clue about the roadblocks that would challenge my dreams, desires, and efforts when I stepped over the invisible line, which I did.

I got pregnant.

No matter that I'd been married for six years. That wasn't the point. It was unacceptable for a professional woman to be pregnant. Period.

Slowly, my house of cards came tumbling down. One thing, then another.

The next decades saw me through a divorce, being social, an illegal abortion, a supportive remarriage, Dad dying, Mom dying, husband dying. At the same time, the decades gave me an adventurous life working a smorgasbord of interesting jobs in various locations, raising children, mostly by myself, and the joy of participating in the Back-to-the-Land and New Age movements. A sense of myself.

In the early '90s, I brushed up my education and went to work as a nutritionist with a rural clinic in Kansas. What a jolt! Nutrition wasn't the same anymore. Diets, fast-food restaurants, processed foods in packages. Yikes! Hanging on to my past, I gave Natural Nutrition workshops and counseled clients. I made friends with the local bookstore and read aggressively.

That's when I realized what had happened. The Food and Drug Administration (FDA) had changed the legal definition of food: from food for health to food for profit.

That opened the doors for the industrial food business to market a tsunami of processed foods. With impunity, they did what they wanted. I was catching up as fast as I could, but it overwhelmed me. Even with grassroots movements rising, I couldn't get traction.

A job teaching fitness fell into my lap. I jumped on it, feeling confident having taken aerobics classes and strength training for years. Work was fun. Nice change! I advanced during the next 17 years, teaching many fitness modalities, especially loving yoga.

Still, foods and nutrition were my heart's true love.

I slipped back into nutrition via the internet with a website and a newsletter sharing natural nutrition and brain and body fitness, with the tagline, "Its Never Too Late to Start Feeling Great," and I wrote a book on healthy aging.

At age 83, I retired from teaching fitness to write this autobiography.

I have a wealth of history to share with you featuring changing attitudes and practices around food, nutrition, and women's lives. I share forgotten facts and fresh insights; ways to identify slick advertising and wrong science; how to pick your "experts," how to choose a diet for yourself with confidence.

Intertwined throughout I share those prickly roadblocks designed to keep women in their place. I share secrets I've held for a lifetime, enabling me to narrate, sometimes in detail, the patriarchal-sanctioned abuses that robbed me of my full potential as a professional woman and as a human being.

Uncanny correlations unfold when taking a bird's eye view of the mistreatment of women and marketing of false food over these past 85 years.

Now, the distractions of these uncertain times create an opening for action to reclaim our health and ourselves, to turn The Bite of History around. The shift has already begun.

It All Started Here

THE BITE OF HISTORY

The Formative Years

Chapter 1: Early Woman Training

When I was born, Dad said, "Damn, a girl!" Mom smiled and said nothing. He told Mom, "We'll try again." Mom smiled and said nothing.

When I was about six months old, my folks moved us to Flagstaff, way up in the mountains. At first, we lived in an attic room above the town's only drugstore.

Dad had landed a job as Head of the Science Department at Arizona State Teachers College, except that the state had no money to pay him because of The Depression. But old Mr. Babbitt owned the town's general store and gave government workers half on the dollar, betting the state would eventually make good on the other half. I understand that never happened. Too bad. Everybody appreciated Mr. Babbitt's kindness and generosity.

My parents found a big old house to rent at the top of the hill on Leroux Street, only a few blocks from town, and we moved in. We came in by way of an open porch on the north side into the living room that had a couch and two big soft chairs. Straight ahead was a telephone high up on the wall where kids couldn't reach. We only used it on holidays or birthdays. The dining room had a big table for eating, Mom's treadle Singer sewing machine, and the ironing board. The kitchen was big with a little table for sitting and eating snacks.

There were four bedrooms, one for Mom and Dad, two to rent out to college girls, and one for me. I always had five or six everyday dresses in my closet and a lovely Sunday dress, like the one with an emerald green velvet bodice, cream-colored lace collar, slightly puffed sleeves and a soft cotton skirt. Behind my bedroom was a big screened porch where everyone did laundry. There was an agitating washing machine with a wringer, deep tubs with a washboard, clotheslines and drying racks.

When I was 2 and a half, Dr. Fronsky came to our house one evening to help Mom deliver her baby. That meant Mom was going to let the baby out. She'd been keeping that baby in her stomach for a long time. I knew it was true because I'd felt it kicking from inside her stomach. Two of Mom's friends came in to help. They made me stand out of the way, but I could still see. After Dad had set up some lights, he stayed out of the way with me.

After a while, Mom's friends got up and were hovering around her. They started telling her things like, "Keep breathing." One wiped her forehead with wet cloths. Another held her hand. Mom was usually a soft-spoken sort of lady, but not that night. She hollered and grunted and carried on something terrible. In a while, as if Mom couldn't hear, everyone got real loud giving her instructions to breathe and push and so on. I got so excited, I got right down into the middle of it. Dad pulled me back. Hurt my feelings.

Finally, it happened. Dr. Fronsky pulled, and Mom pushed, and the baby came right out of her pee pee. It was a 'he' and all slimy. They washed him up, put him in a blanket, and gave him to Mom. She snuggled him up and talked to him quiet-like, and then he behaved. That's how I got my baby brother.

Ruthie lived next door with her really old mom and dad. We became good friends, sharing Jell-O, cookies, and secrets. We even made an igloo one winter by tunneling under the snow on the north side of our house.

Whenever I got real busy playing outside, I would just drop my drawers, squat, and pee. When I was around 3, Mom saw me one day. She ran out of the house screaming at me, "What do you think you're doing?"

"Peeing."

"You can't do that out here! Someone might see you!" She dragged me into the house by the arm and took me to the cupboard where she kept my brother's diapers and got one down. "Here," she said, "If you can't hold it long enough to come into the bathroom, you'll have to wear one of these when you go out to play." Humiliating.

Another time I was showing off my ringworm to the neighbors. Mom got mad about that, too. "But it's on my tummy!"

"You should never lift up your dress in public."

Summer weekends we'd picnic along the stream down in Oak Creek Canyon. The trip down off the mesa scared me. There was hardly enough room for cars to pass each other without the outside one slipping off and down to the canyon below. But I never let on how frightened I was.

At the bottom of the canyon, you could hear the stream going over the rocks and the leaves rustling in the yellow and red trees. Sometimes we'd see a man trying to catch a fish.

Dad would build a fire and Mom would put on the blue enamel percolator for coffee. Even at home, she'd let me have coffee with canned milk and sugar. Later, we'd cook hot dogs on a stick and roast marshmallows.

On the way home, we always stopped at the big dance hall in Sedona for gas and an orange Nehi soft drink. I learned a lesson there. I had my allowance, five nickels: two for the church and three for me. They had a nickel slot machine, and Dad said I could play it. I didn't win three times, but was so sure I would the next time, I played the two nickels for the church. I lost again. Dad laughed. I was embarrassed that I had no money for the plate.

Three times, I had to be quarantined. First with the three-day measles and a high fever, then with chicken pox, which itched like crazy but you couldn't scratch or they would spread, and again with the mumps. The mumps was the worst; they hurt. I had to put ice packs on both sides of my face just below the ears and slurp soup up with a straw even though I wasn't hungry. Each time, Dr. Fronsky put a sign on the front door; no one could come in or go out, even Dad. He went on the porch every day bringing groceries; Mom would put clean clothes out for him and a lunch bucket. When infantile paralysis (polio) happened one summer, the movie theater and swimming pool closed. Mom and Dad took me to Santa Barbara to live with Gramma so it couldn't get me. Some kids weren't as lucky as I was.

In second or third grade, I got the "real" measles." I had a high fever and a cough and my eyes hurt. I had to stay in bed for two or three weeks. The blinds were pulled so that no light could come in; if you looked at the light, you could go blind or get other terrible diseases or die. Mom was the only person who ever came in.

When I was five, we moved to a teeny-tiny house on Beaver Street just up from the Episcopal Church. I had a loud "pitch-perfect" soprano voice, so I got to sing in the real church choir, the 11 o'clock one. I sang for many years until they found out I hadn't been baptized. The church people said I could sing if my parents would come in to talk to them, but my parents didn't want to. So I didn't get to sing anymore.

In late summer, I had to have my tonsils out so I could start school. While I was in the hospital, our old dog, Schnapps, got run over. I couldn't cry because my throat hurt. Mom said he was old, and that it was time for him to go to dog heaven. Not crying was hard.

But having tonsillitis wasn't all bad. I stayed in bed and played with my blocks and painted metal British soldiers. Mom read to me and fed me bone broth. Dad brought ice cream. It wasn't long before I was ready to go to school.

Kindergarten was fun except for old Mrs. Docksdater fussing at me all the time. "Caroline, pick up your feet." I think it was the Buster Browns that Mom made me wear: "They're sturdy, and they'll give you strong legs and feet." But they were ugly boys' shoes, and they stuck to the floor.

Funny how some of the problems of youth come back when we get old. Sometimes my feet stick to the floor now, and I'm getting clumsy again.

Real soon, we moved again, this time to a better house on the corner of Elm and Agassiz. I had a room upstairs where I could see the meadow across the street. On warm days, I would lie down in it, watching the changing shapes of the puffy clouds against the turquoise sky. I was still as a mouse so I could hear the butterflies and the rustling of the grass. At night up in my bedroom, I'd opened the windows and curtains. I could see the stars and feel the light gusts of air off the mesa behind us, listen to the pines moving and breathe in their pungent fragrance.

While we were on Elm Street, Dad and some of his students built a rock house just up the hill. We moved in. It was better because I could hear the trains' clickety-clacking along with their whistles blowing. Hobos on their way to California to work in the orchards would sometimes make their way up the hill to our house. They'd sit on our back stoop eating soup Mom made for them. Dad said we couldn't afford to feed them, but Mom did it anyhow.

Chapter 2: Now That You Are Six

I was already in first grade by the time I turned six and I was allowed to ride the school bus. In the evenings the neighborhood kids would play hide 'n seek, kick the can, and red rover. That was SO much fun. On weekends, we played cops and robbers among the boulders and trees. Some kids had cap guns; others made guns cut from forked tree branches.

"Now that you are six, you can help me with dinner," said my mother with a twinkle in her eye. My heart jumped. "You can make the salad. We'll have a carrot-raisin salad tonight." My heart jumped again because that meant I got to use a knife. I'd been helping with dinner for a long time by setting the table. "Presentation is everything," Mom would say.

Meals had to be attractive, inviting, with a clean tablecloth and napkins folded across and then long-ways so that an open tip would be at the bottom next to the plate. Napkins were on the left side so they would be easy to grab. The floral decoration on the dinner plate faced the person eating. Two forks went on the left, the dinner fork inside, the salad fork outside, and the spoon was on the right. The salad plate went above the forks and the milk glass above the spoon. I was pretty good at knowing just what to do.

For the salad, I scrubbed the carrots with a brush. Then, one by one, I pressed the point of each carrot against the breadboard, with the big end in my hand and my index finger down on the carrot to hold it steady. With the knife held at just the right angle, I scraped the carrot clean of dirt and skin, rotating it until it was clean all around. After doing them all, I lay them on the breadboard. I cut off the fat ends first and then the pointy ends. Finally, I cut each carrot long-ways into fours, then sideways into finger-long logs.

* * *

Everyone helped each other back then. Mom worked for the town's only doctor, Dr. Fronsky. She helped in the office and every Friday she checked the prostitutes on the other side of the railroad tracks for venereal disease. She was paid 75 dollars a month, pretty good for the times. And Dr. Fronsky gave us free house calls if we were sick. He'd come with his black bag and stethoscope. Anytime I had a sore throat or something, he would find a little bottle of tiny, sweet, round pills in his bag to make me feel better. They did.

Another good thing about Dr. Fronsky was that he gave Mom the free samples of Alka-Seltzer, which Dad liked, and of cod-liver oil for me and my brother to keep us healthy. Mom made us take a spoonful every day, which made us gag, especially the orange-flavored one.

Dad made a milk run every week for several neighbors and us because we had a car. The dairy was out on the north side of town. For each family, he picked up a galvanized can of milk, cottage cheese, and butter. Folks would let the milk "rest" for a day or two because some were sensitive and would get a bellyache if the milk was too fresh. At home, we poured ours from the can into big jars and kept them cool on the back porch if it was winter or in the refrigerator if it was summer. Near the end of the week, Mom set some of the milk out on the back of the stove to clabber and then made a pound cake with lots of eggs and butter.

We gave some of our milk to Beatrice who was about 18 and stayed with my little brother and me while Mom and Dad were at work. On Saturdays, Beatrice and her mother brought us a basket of tamales they made of corn mush with a brown streak of meat juice running down the middle, and wrapped in cornhusks. Yummy. Mom let both Beatrice and her mother take a bath in our tub.

* * *

The four finished carrot-raisin salads were beautiful. A bed of bite-sized pieces of iceberg lettuce was under each one. Five carrot pieces pointed out from the middle in a star-shaped ring. About ten raisins, soaked in warm water first so they would be soft, were scattered in the center of the ring. On top, I plopped a spoonful of mayonnaise down in such a way that it looked like a small mountain with a pointy top. I placed them on the table just above the forks.

Plates and serving bowls went into the plate warmer on the side of our wood-burning stove while we poured the milk and set out the salt and pepper shakers, bread and butter.

Mom called us to dinner at five o'clock, when everyone else in town ate theirs, too. We came right away and sat in our places. Mom and Dad sat across from each other; John and I sat across from each other, too.

Mom placed the warmed plates in front of Dad and then the bowls of food. Dad served each of us starting with Mom, then me, then John and then himself. We were silent for a moment. We children could start eating after the grown-ups had had their first bite. The carrot salads made our dinner of pot roast, mashed potatoes with butter, and home-canned string beans look quite elegant.

Mom and Dad talked about the events of the day and the war in Europe. Then Dad asked each of us children to tell about our day. I talked a lot; John didn't say much.

Our pot roast was from a half-frozen cow that hung in our shed during Flagstaff's long winter. We had a pig hanging, too. Dad would saw off a piece of meat for the next day's meal and bring it inside to thaw in the kitchen sink. In the summer, we ate mostly egg or cheese dishes.

Mom tried to garden in the rocky soil on the south side of the house, but things didn't grow well there. But we had chickens, so we bartered eggs for vegetables with neighbors who lived down the hill and had better soil. We would can vegetables in season for the whole year. We kept them cool on our back porch, which had no heat but didn't freeze either. String beans, peas, corn, tomatoes, tomato sauce, and pickles.

Fruit didn't grow well in mile-high Flagstaff, so we didn't have much, not enough to can. At Christmas, John and I each got an orange in the bottom of our stockings. Aunt Lorraine lived in California and sent them along with a big burlap bag of almonds and another of walnuts. John and I had the job of cracking and shelling the nuts, which made me sneeze and my eyes water.

Mom let me shoot the almond's insides out. She blanched them just until the brown inner skins barely came loose from the naked nut inside, then set them out to cool for a minute. Holding one firmly between my thumb and index finger, halfway back with the pointy end forward, I'd squeeze till the white nut flew out of its skin. Ping! Hit the inside of the Pyrex mixing bowl.

I helped Mom bake the Christmas treats: Kifflen (a tea cookie rolled in powdered sugar), Pfeffer Nusse (a crisp, lemon and cardamom almond cookie), Lebkuchen, (a gingerbread cookie), Nutsenstrudel (a long nut-paste layered yeast roll) and cinnamon nuts, a family favorite.

Christmas was the best time of the year for eating. We had big meals, often with family or friends. Plus, we had cookies and pies and eggnog. Aunt Lorraine sent a whole pound of See's candy for Christmas Eve. The rest of the year, we only had dessert on Sundays, like pudding or custard or pie, a cake on birthdays and pumpkin pie with whipped cream at Thanksgiving.

Another reason Christmas was the best time was that we were out of school, and there was always snow, sometimes a lot. The best hill for sledding was over on Leroux Street in front of our old house. It was steep and ran nearly all the way down into town. Everyone came with their Flexible Flyers to sled on a packed-snow day, kids and grown-ups, too, all bundled up in snowsuits, a warm hat, a muffler, big boots, and warm gloves. We'd burn an old tire at the top of the hill for a bit of warmth.

That Christmas I asked Santa to bring me an Erector Set. One of the boys from school had one; I had watched him make buildings and bridges with metal girders and cranks, screws and a screwdriver. Dad told me that Erector Sets were for boys. Christmas Eve, we sang songs and Mom read *The Night Before Christmas*, and we went to bed early.

Every year on Christmas morning, my brother and I each had to eat a big bowl of oatmeal with cream or a big hunk of butter and brown sugar before we could go into the living room to see what Santa had left. John got a red and yellow dump truck; I got a Diddy Doll, a soft rubber doll with a hole in its mouth and another between its legs. You put water in the little bottle that came with it, stuck the bottle in the doll's mouth hole and squeezed. The water came right out of the hole on the bottom and got its diaper wet. Boring. I was sure then that Dad was Santa Claus because I figured that a real Santa would bring the toy that kids had asked for.

But it was OK because I got a turquoise sidewalk bike, too, and John got a red Radio Flyer wagon, so it was a good Christmas.

Chapter 3: School - Finding My Bottom

By Christmas, I was starting not to like first grade. I had memorized Dick and Jane from when others read it aloud, but I couldn't read it. And Miss Roseberry was too fast with the flash cards; the letters on the cards didn't connect with words for me. When we had tests, the kids who got the answers right got a sticker on their paper to show their parents, but I never got one. They were horses or cows or pigs and were so cute.

One day when everyone was out on the playground for lunch, I came in to go to the bathroom, and our room was empty. (Each classroom had a bathroom.)

Quick-like, I pushed Miss Roseberry's chair up against the chalkboard and climbed up from there onto the bookcase and stood on it with tippy-toes so I could reach the top of the chalkboard where Miss Roseberry kept the stickers.

I could feel them. I slipped one off, climbed down, put the chair back, went into the bathroom, and looked at my sticker. It was a cow. I would rather have had a horse, but it would do.

That night I licked the back, put it on my paper, and gave it to Mom and Dad at dinner. They looked at it, then at each other and Mom said, "I wonder why your paper has a sticker on it when there are several mistakes." I didn't get whipped but got a very long lecture. Next day, Mom took me to school and talked with Miss Roseberry. Miss Roseberry told her about my trouble reading and paying attention. They decided I should sit in the front row.

That worked for a while, sort of, but by second grade, I was a problem again. On our Christmas trip to the grandmas that year, Mom pointed out the car window and said, "Look at the gorgeous moon coming up over the mountain." I couldn't see the moon; I couldn't even see the mountain. We went to see an eye doctor right away. By the time we headed back to Flagstaff, I had round, sturdy, metal-framed eyeglasses. They were hideous.

I didn't care if I couldn't see. My life was over. The only kid in school who had to wear glasses. And I still couldn't read. And the kids teased me. Especially one skinny boy.

We girls were playing hopscotch on the tennis court at lunchtime when he came circling around us, pointing at me and singing, "Hey, four-eyes… ugly four-eyes." I lost it. I rushed at him pushing him hard to the ground, jumped on top of him, and bammed his head into the asphalt. He screamed. The girls were screaming, too, "Get off." I got scared because if I got up and let him go, he would probably beat me up. Suddenly, the playground teacher grabbed my arm and jerked me up. It felt like she had pulled my arm off my body. The school nurse came running over to see the boy; I was dragged into the principal's office.

The boy was OK—after a week or so. I cried a lot (in private). I didn't want to be a "toughie." I didn't want to wear glasses. I didn't want to be teased. I didn't want to be the dumbest one in class.

From then on, I avoided every reading class possible throughout my school years. How? By signing up for, and taking, science and hands-on courses like cooking and chemistry. Some, but not much reading required. A natural for me. Funny how seemingly trivial events in life can be germane to one's life journey.

Chapter 4: Meals at Gramma's

Twice a year, at Christmas and summer, we'd pile in our old car and drive Route 66 from Flagstaff to California to spend a week visiting Dad's family in San Jose and another week with Mom's family in Santa Barbara.

The big, old Victorian house in San Jose had a sweet-smelling backyard garden filled with vegetables, fruit trees, and berries. Augusta, the cook and housekeeper, picked each day's vegetables early in the morning. I loved to help her; shelling peas was my favorite, the way they just shot out as I slid my thumb long-ways down the inside of the pod. They usually landed in the pot.

A big kitchen and a small, room-sized pantry were just inside the back-porch door. The pantry housed a big icebox that was taller than the grown-ups and had two doors on the front that opened out. When I stood in front of it and stretched my arms out wide, I couldn't reach the sides.

Inside, on the bottom, was a big pan where the ice went. The iceman came every few days. With giant tongs, he would bring in a big block of ice and put it in the pan. Then he would get another and put it on top. He gave us kids chips of ice from his truck. The milkman delivered butter, milk, and eggs before dawn. I don't know where the meat came from, but there was always plenty for meals.

At one time, Grandpa sold ribbons in the department store downtown and fell in love with Gramma then. But Great Grandpa wouldn't let him marry her until he "made something of himself." So he went to doctor school for a lot of years, and when he got to be a pediatrician, they were married. She was 39 and had to have his last name. She went from Susan Cory to Susan Hablutzel—hard to say.

It was OK for Great Grandpa to be like that since he was a self-made man himself. In 1848 at the age of 22, he had left Mexico, Missouri, walking the Oregon Trail to the Pacific and down the California Trail to

San Francisco in search of gold, with his fresh new doctor's certificate and black bag in hand. Great Granpa didn't make it as a gold miner, but with the booming population, he made lots of money doctoring. He was one of the first doctors in the territory. Streets and schools are named after him, still.

All the important food was kept in the icebox: meat, a freshly plucked chicken, and milk. You didn't open the doors unless you had to. The hydrator, which was cool but not cold, was attached to the side of the icebox. That's where the butter and vegetables lived.

Mealtime was formal. When Augusta was ready to serve, she came out of the kitchen and rang the little silver bell with a high-pitched ding, ding, ding. Everyone came into the dining room and quietly took their appointed seat at the long table. Grandpa sat at one end, and Gramma sat at the opposite end. John and I had tall chairs with ladder rungs to climb. Once we were up, Dad or Mom pushed in our chairs close to the table. Next, we all took the napkins out of the napkin rings and placed them neatly on our laps. No one talked.

When everyone was ready, Grandpa rang the bell to let Augusta know she could serve the food. When she finished bringing in all the serving dishes and placing them correctly in front of Grandpa, he began to serve each plate, which we passed around, to Gramma first, then her sister, Aunt Sarah, then Dad, Mom, us children, and himself last. Grandpa shook a lot, so it took a very long time. After he offered the prayer, we could eat.

I can't remember much of what we ate there, except for my birthday morning. I was allowed to have six raspberries in my fruit dish instead of 5 because I was now 6.

Only the grown-ups talked during the meal unless one of them asked John or me a question. We had to be sure to swallow before answering.

My other grandmother in Santa Barbara had a garden, too, but smaller. The icebox and hydrator were smaller. So was their house. It was bright and friendly with sunny windows and comfy furniture. It sat on a hillside overlooking the ocean and was covered all around with vines and sweet-smelling flowers. Gramma had flowers in the kitchen, too, and a canary named Peetie and a tall tin of chewy lemon sugar cookies under the bench in the breakfast nook.

Mom's older sister, Auntie Lorraine, lived there and took care of Gramma. She was a first-grade school teacher and had a rumble seat car.

Mom told me that Gramma had been beautiful with blonde hair and a "peaches and cream" complexion when she was 17 and came to America so she wouldn't have to be in the German army for two years. Germany had just taken Schleswig-Holstein from Denmark, and Gramma's dad was so angry that he put each of his six kids on a boat for America as they turned 17. From New York, Gramma took the Southern Pacific Railroad to Tucson (that would have been 1892), and then a stagecoach from Tucson to Tombstone where she had an uncle. But when they got to Tombstone, her uncle had just died. Even though she spoke "broken English," a kind family took her in. It wasn't long before a handsome bachelor, a Mining Inspector for that area, spotted her. He scooped her up. They married and moved up the road to Bisbee, which is where Mom was born.

I thought Gramma was still pretty. She had blush cheeks and a streak of blonde hair starting just to the side of her widow's peak. She braided it and coiled the braid around her head several times. She hummed a lot, especially while she cooked, which was most of the time.

Gramma was a magical cook with her Danish farm-life heritage and hands-on ways. My favorite dinner was fluffy meatloaf, mashed potatoes with lots of butter, baked carrots with cheese grated and melted on top, yeast rolls with butter and jam, fresh cold milk, and for dessert, she'd make applesauce with thick cream on top.

Uncles, aunts, cousins, and friends were always coming by to visit and often stayed for dinner. Mealtime felt like a celebration with storytelling, laughing, and even we kids were welcome to join in.

Santa Barbara was the BEST place to visit. We'd go to the beach, to the duck pond and up into the mountains for a picnic. But, nothing was as exciting as the day Uncle Tommy took us to see the new supermarket.

Chapter 5: The Supermarket

Sometimes, when visiting the grandmas in California, we would stop first to visit with my mom's sister, Elizabeth, in Compton, California. It was a small town then, at the end of the track for the Red Cars. There were not many houses, but mostly big open fields where stinging nettles would get your legs if you went out to pet the horses.

My uncle Tommy was Chief of Police. He gave John and me each a real silver dollar every time we came to visit. On this day, he took us to see a supermarket. "It's the first one in Southern California," he said proudly. He told us that small markets had been growing up all over the country, usually selling either canned and dry foods or just meat. But supermarkets were coming in style; they were so big they could sell everything in just one store.

I thought he was talking about a general store like old Mr. Babbitt's store in Flagstaff. But this supermarket was as big as a football field, it seemed. Tall with giant doors and lights outside that you could see from a long way off.

Stepping inside just took my breath away. It was so bright and shiny, I had to cover my eyes for a minute. The coolness was indescribable, like stepping into another country near the North Pole, or into a deep cave, like at Meteor Crater. It made my skin tingle. And SO much food. Not just canned and dry foods, but fresh vegetables and fruits on tables all around. Things that had to be kept cool like milk and cheese were kept in special cabinets along the walls. There were rows of refrigerator cases with packages of frozen food. Even meat. Even creamsicles and fudge bars. Miles of Nehi, Root Beer, and Coca-Cola. More toilet paper and paper towels than I had ever seen, even different kinds. Even soap and cold cream and perfume.

John and I walked, sliding our fingers along the metal cases. It was like a fairyland.

That was our last trip to California before the war came when we had to move to Albuquerque.

Moving Around

Chapter 6: War Time in Albuquerque

We moved from Flagstaff to Albuquerque the summer I finished fourth grade. Dad was picked to work on a secret government project for the Navy at Sandia Base. We rented a new tract house on the east edge of town near the end of the runway at Kirtland Air Force Base. No grass or trees. No neighbors. It was hot and dry. The wind blew every afternoon, and sand got all over everything, even crept in around the edges of the windows and dirtied up the windowsills. The B-29s flew out on training missions around 4 am and came back just at dinner time. The P-38s flew during the day. What a noise! Mom cried. Dad said it was because she was pregnant, that she'd be okay.

Mom enrolled John and me into Bandelier Elementary on the edge of the base. I was the only kid in school who wore glasses, but I wasn't mad about it anymore. Worse was that the fifth-grade kids could already write in cursive. Mom talked with my new teacher about my problem, and she seemed to understand. She sent a small chalkboard home with me so that I could practice and some easy booklets to read about volcanoes and lizards.

Baby Benjamin Cory, named after Great Grandpa Benjamin Cory, was born October 12th, 1942. He was so cute that we called him Benjie. Soon Mom was happy again. I got to cook and do laundry and help take care him.

The next summer we moved into an older, friendlier house closer in town. John and I could still go to Bandelier, and it was only a mile from the Junior High School so I could bike there when I went into seventh grade.

Dad was able to put in a garden, as the soil was OK. Not good, but OK. His winter plants came up a little scrawny. I had an idea and thought I could help Dad out.

I had learned in school that farmers were using chemical fertilizers containing nitrogen to make plants grow better and produce more tomatoes, wheat, and corn. I also learned that urine contained nitrogen. So, real early one morning, I secretly peed into a bucket, added water and snuck out to give a little to each of Dad's plants. In two days, they were all dead. I never told anyone about that until now.

Years later when I took Agronomy in college, I learned about chemical fertilizers and finally understood why the plants had died.

Dad spread cow manure all over his garden. The plants came up fine in the spring.

When Benjie got older, Mom weaned him to formula in a bottle. It was my job to make it. First, I cleaned and steamed the bottles, caps, and nipples to be sure there were no germs. I made the formula in a pot on the stove with canned milk and an equal amount of water and poured in some Karo. I knew how much without having to measure it.

It was wartime, a strange time for everyone. Creepiest of all were the air-raid drills because you never knew if they were real. When the siren went off, we'd fast-walk single-file from our schoolrooms, into the hall, and lie face down on the floor against the wall with my nose to the baseboard and arms covering my head, thinking I might die. Wondering if John was in the hall by his room and scared. If Mom and Benjie were taking cover. When the all-clear sounded, we filed back into our rooms and were quiet for a while.

Every week I bought a 10-cent war stamp and saved it in a book until there were enough to get a 25-dollar war bond. There was competition among classes to see which class could dress a GI Joe first. GI Joe was a tall cardboard guy that we would 'dress' with paper cut-out clothes. Each clothing part had a cost, like a shirt sleeve cost so many war stamps. Took a while to finish dressing one GI Joe.

One never really gets over these things.

John and I would listen to the radio at seven o'clock for an hour: Red Skelton, Fibber McGee and Molly, The Shadow, The Lone Ranger, Inner Sanctum Mystery, or Lux Radio Theater. At eight o'clock, everyone went to bed.

My friends and I were Girl Scouts. We knitted wool yarn into four-inch by four-inch squares that a ladies group made into blankets for our troops. We walked the alleys searching trash cans for tin foil to use in making ammunition, wrapping it up in a tight ball, and turning it in at scout meetings. Everyone saved paper and fat, but I can't remember why.

I was obsessed with earning Girl Scout badges, everything from woodworking to first aid. I had badges all up the sleeves of my uniform and on a sash across my front. I was a 1st Class Scout, of course.

Many ordinary items had been rationed or were scarce, so meal preparation was a challenge. Rationed food included meat, bacon, lard, milk, butter, cheese, sugar, tea, jam, biscuits, breakfast cereals, eggs, and canned and dried fruit. Every month we would get our family's issue of stamps to buy food. There were also stamps for gas and other things I can't remember. Gramma in San Jose and Aunt Sarah would send us their shoe stamps, so John and I never had to go without shoes like some kids.

Since metal was scarce, typical coins such as pennies, nickels, and dimes were replaced by tokens: hard, little paper-like disks that had the denomination pressed into them, different colors for different denominations.

Fresh vegetables and fruit were in short supply. So, like most people, we had a "victory garden" and backyard chickens. Since the chickens were for food, we weren't allowed to give them names.

On a Saturday, Dad would hold a chicken upside down by its feet so it would go to sleep, then smack its neck fast and hard across the edge of a sturdy metal garbage can, lay it sideways over a flat stump, and chop off its head with a hand ax. When the headless chicken quit flopping around, Dad would hang it by its feet from the clothesline so the blood would drain out into a little bucket he put on a stool. Mom used the drippings to make gravy or added them to bones to make broth. After the chicken finished draining, she would hold it upside down by its feet and dip it into a pot of boiling water for about two minutes. The feathers would loosen so that we could pull them out better. We had to pluck out the pin feathers with tweezers. Everybody helped.

We had either stewed chicken with potatoes, carrots and onions or baked chicken with stale bread dressing made with onions and celery mixed in with broth. Always a potato, a vegetable, and milk for John and me.

I made our lunches for school: white bread sandwiches filled with egg salad, tuna salad, peanut butter and jelly, diced black olives, which made the bread wet and gummy, or Vienna sausages, cut in half long-ways and lined up. And always a thermos of soup and maybe an apple.

During World War II, the dairy industry sent practically all of its butter to "our boys" overseas. At home, we used lard for our bread spread. It was gross. Soon oleo showed up in the store. Researchers had figured out a way to change corn oil into white blocks that looked like lard.

Soon a little packet of dark orange coloring came with each block. It was my job to mix it in. It was easier if I warmed the oleo first. Tasted different than lard, but not any better, and it felt like wax in my mouth. It didn't "bloom" with a delicious mouth-watering aroma like butter. I wouldn't eat oleo; rather just eat bread, potatoes, and veggies by themselves. Mom said I should just learn to accept what was . . . not be so picky, so stubborn about it.

When "our boys" came home after the war, so did butter. Oleo lost sales. The oleo companies started coloring the oleo themselves and packed it in quarter-pound units. Still, sales slumped. Pretty soon, we heard, "Use Margarine! It's made from corn, and everyone knows that vegetable oil is better for you than animal fat." Brilliant! Sales went up. Some people stayed with oleo. It's still around, even though we now know that, in fact, vegetable oil is the unhealthy option.

Interesting that 15 years later I was part of a research team looking for a way to create butter flavor.

Chapter 7: Teen Drama

Finally, it happened. A dark spot in my underpants. We'd had a slide show presentation about it in seventh-grade PE. Four slides to be exact. Projected up on a screen. The window shades were pulled so the boys couldn't peek in. I only remember the sketch of a uterus. An uncomfortable teacher tried to explain what happens and why. No questions allowed.

I told Mom about the spot. She said matter-of-factly, "Everything you need is on the floor of the bedroom closet behind the shoes." I found a box of Kotex and an elastic belt contraption. I took a Kotex and the belt into the bathroom and figured out what to do with them. Pretty simple, though incredibly uncomfortable, being thick, too wide, and too long, like tying a small pillow between your thighs onto your hips. I practiced walking with it on.

Belts were phased out in the 1970s; napkins didn't come in sizes and styles until even later.

Mom made me buy my own. "Just go to the drugstore and tell the pharmacist what you want. That's all."

I went and with a red face and tied tongue, spit it out. "I need Kotex and an . . . um . . . um . . . the elastic-like thing that goes around here," I said sliding my hands around my upper hips. He was a kind, stone-faced man. He got them from the shelf, put them in a brown bag, and told me the price.

People didn't talk about "women's personal private affairs" in my day. Ever. We had no access to information about menstruation, sex, or birth control. No books, not in the newspapers or magazines, not on the radio. Still nothing, even when TV arrived. The personal computer was 45 years away. We were "protected" from knowing the culture of the times, though I did the forbidden: took a hand mirror and looked "down there." How strange. Where does the pee come out? The baby? The poopie hole was obvious.

And so it was that by the end of my twelfth year, I was well-rooted into my family traditions, had insights into my strengths and limitations, and best of all, I was now a woman.

We were going to move back to Flagstaff after the war, but Gramma in San Jose got cancer, so we moved there instead. Grandpa had died, so had Augusta. Gramma and Aunt Sarah were the only ones left in the big house. Everyone's lives changed when we moved in with them. I don't remember much about it.

Except that I was in ninth grade at Jefferson Junior High School, where we had PE twice a day, 30 minutes mid-morning and 30 minutes mid-afternoon, plus an hour for lunch. I got my first boyfriend, Robert, and wore his Future Farmers of America jacket, royal blue corduroy with an FFA medallion on the front right side, stitched in gold thread.

That summer, I got my first job: a carhop at The Dutch Creamery, just a short walk from home. I earned 37 cents an hour and got to wear a Dutch-girl outfit: blue dress, mid-calf, topped with a white apron and a traditional starched white bonnet with wings.

An older man parked his car way out in the parking lot every day. I noticed how he watched me as I brought his tray to him. One day when I picked up his tray, I found a five-dollar tip. I told the manager. He brought me indoors to work the counter.

The trouble with that was that I couldn't keep track of the orders and who got what. It reminded me of first grade. So the manager put me in the kitchen making sandwiches, which was fun, especially the slippery mayo, avocado, and lettuce ones. And delicious; I got to eat one for free each day.

We didn't write down orders, and there were no calculators in those days; you had to remember it all in your head.

Robert worked on his dad's alfalfa farm that summer and I spent time just hanging out with him. That's when I felt my first "urgings." I snuggled with him and got my first kiss. So tender; so sweet, it made my heart pound and my face flush. Up in the loft of the hay barn one afternoon, he asked if I wanted to see his dickie. I'd only seen my little brothers' dickies, and I caught a glimpse of Dad's once as he walked naked from his bathroom to his bedroom.

I said, "Yes." Barely breathing, I trembled as Robert unzipped his Levis. It was much bigger and nicer than I'd imagined and soft to the touch. He was proud of it. He lifted my skirt and put it on my thigh. That's when I panicked.

I'd heard the girls in PE talking about how there was a hole at the end of dickies where a messy blob would come out, and it had sperm in it so tiny you couldn't see them, and they would slither up into your privates and make you pregnant. A few years earlier, I had lost my "cherry" crashing a boy's bike into a curb. My private place hit the bar so hard that I bled. My friend, Charlotte, told me your cherry was the plug that kept you from getting pregnant. So if you lost it, the sperm could get up there easily.

I told Robert that I didn't want to see his dickie anymore and to please, put it away, which he did.

Amazingly, Gramma's cancer got better. Dad got her and Aunt Sarah a small house in Santa Clara near her sister, Aunt Harriet and Uncle Dolph. They had a little fruit ranch, berries, and plums. He got them moved in just in the nick of time. A grand position was offered to Dad: Vice President of Research for United Gas of America, in Shreveport, Louisiana. We packed up again and went.

* * *

It was a long trip. I watched the clouds roll by, the fields, the towns, quietly crying. I missed Robert so, so much that I could hardly think of anything else, particularly of that magical moment in the hayloft. After a while, I started wondering about that. Was it true that sperm came out in a blob? That they were microscopic? Could they have come out without a blob, gone up my leg and gotten into my privates? That was silly. But, what if? Well, I at least knew that you could tell in a month, that if you missed your period, you were pregnant.

Shreveport was hot and sticky when we arrived in late August. We found a suitable tract house a few blocks from John's school and a bus-ride to mine, C. E. Byrd High School, which started in a week. I helped Mom get the new house set up and watched the calendar. The month came and went, and nothing happened. No period. Now I was getting scared. Another three days, no period. Oh, dear God. Was it true? What should I do? What can I do?

Six weeks passed, and I knew I had to tell my Mom that I was pregnant. So I did and made her promise she wouldn't tell Dad. She turned white and fell into a chair staring at me.

"What can we do?" I asked. She couldn't talk.

Dad came home early, walked in, and stared at us. "What's wrong?"

"Caroline's pregnant," Mom bawled out, now crying.

"Oh, my God," he yelled, turned on me with a litany of loud, accusative questions: "Who?" "When?" "How?" "Stupid Kids!" and stormed out of the room, then came back in shouting the same questions.

I just couldn't answer, didn't know what to say. I ran to my room, threw myself on the bed, and wept.

After a while, Dad came into my room and sat on the edge of my bed. "Are you sure, Sweetheart?"

"No, Dad, I'm not."

"Tell me how it happened."

"I can't; I just can't. But he didn't hurt me."

His eyes searched for mine; I looked down. "You rest. I'm going to figure out what to do."

The next day, Dad found out that a doctor lived in the house behind us. They had talked, and the doctor agreed to give me a rabbit test. I crossed the backyards to his place and knocked. We sat at the kitchen table and talked. He was soft-spoken and showed no judgment as I told him exactly what had happened. "Sometimes women miss their periods for other reasons," he said. "It can be from stress, illness, or sometimes for no particular reason. We'll do the Rabbit Test to find out for sure."

He gave me a paper cup to collect a small amount of pee. That was it. He told me he'd have the results in three days, that I was to go home and not worry.

The rabbit test is an early pregnancy test developed in 1931.

Urine from a woman in the early months of pregnancy is injected into a female rabbit's bloodstream. The rabbit's ovaries enlarge a few days later due to a hormone secreted in the presence of a fertilized egg. The rabbit has to be opened up to find out if her ovaries have enlarged or not. Modern pregnancy tests still depend upon the same hormone; however, current lab techniques spare rabbits.

In three days, Dad told me that the doctor said I wasn't pregnant. A long silence hovered. "I trust you have learned your lesson."

"Yes, sir."

Chapter 8:
High School Southern Style

Shreveport was tough. One other new kid, Jim Elwood, and I were the only "Yankees" in school, meaning neither of us had family who had fought in the Civil War, and those Southern girls weren't nice about that at all. "Your name came up at the meeting on Sunday, but you were blackballed again."

Never mind. I played flute in the band, which was tons of fun, joined the Science Club, and in my senior year, was elected to be a Reserve Officers' Training Corp (R.O.T.C.) Sponsor, 2nd Lieutenant, assigned to the marching band. I got to wear a military uniform: a white skirt, white dress shirt, and black tie. It had a fitted navy jacket with a white lapel with a cross-rifle pin on each side, an R.O.T.C. medallion on the left sleeve, a black belt with a strap that crossed over my right shoulder, a whistle hanging down over my left shoulder, and a classy felt cap. I learned how to shoot and clean an M1 Rifle and make sand maps for military maneuvers.

I was able to slick out of reading classes by taking Theater and got out of taking Spanish by taking Latin, but I couldn't escape Mrs. Davis. She was "no stuff and nonsense." Everyone in the class learned grammar and writing, even me. What I noticed was that writing was a whole lot easier than reading, which gave me hope! She was the best teacher I ever had.

All the girls took Home Economics, sewing first semester and cooking the second semester. In sewing, we made a potholder and an apron. In cooking, we made oatmeal first and then other menu classics.

When my grandson took Food and Nutrition in High School in 2012, they made nachos and s'mores.

We learned about foods: where they came from and how to prepare them. We learned about nutrition, both of the body and its importance in nourishing our future families. I learned The Basic 7 put out by the USDA in 1943 as a nutrition guide promoting foods to help maintain nutritional standards under wartime food rationing. It remained the foundation of my knowledge about food and nutrition through high school and college.

From 1956 until 1992, the United States Department of Agriculture recommended its "Basic Four" food groups. From that time on, a plethora of food groupings from the USDA and others have erupted.

The first two summers, I worked at United Gas at a variety of jobs: filing stock certificates, delivering mail to different offices, typing mistake-proof financial reports on a 180-key typewriter. Thank goodness I was prepared, as I'd already taken typing in school along with most of the girls; but I didn't take shorthand. It made no sense, looked like chicken scratches in the dirt.

The last job I had there was the best—elevator operator. I opened and closed the door with a lever that swung up and over and back again in a half-circle, like the

Senior Prom

23

big hand of a clock going from 9 to 3 and back up and over to 9 again. I wore a stunning uniform, a deep red pleated skirt and tailored warm-beige jacket with a double line of brass buttons down the front, and a perky pill-box hat, red to match the skirt. My shoes were a stylish nut-brown, worn with beige socks that matched the jacket. I got to know every important person who worked there and could greet them by name with a smile.

The Korean War started in June of 1950, the year of my graduation. The senior boys were in the Reserves, so off they went to war as soon as school was over. My friend Junie and I had taken the American Red Cross Life Saving and Instructor classes at the YMCA earlier that spring, so the Shreveport Community Pool snapped us up to not only teach classes but to take on the lifeguard jobs. Thirteen-hour days, 8 am to 9 pm. Exhausting, but exhilarating. I loved it and got a great tan.

Marriage or college was on every girl's mind senior year. Everyone knew if you weren't married by age 30, there was a good chance you would wind up a spinster. Even at 30, in a time when life expectancy for a woman was 62, there wasn't much time left to have and raise children.

Marriage would work out well, as my boyfriend, Perry had a good job driving the local Bird's Eye frozen food truck, and I could work at the United Gas building because of Dad. Perry and I had dated for several years by then. We fished in summer and went duck hunting on Caddo Lake on weekends. We went to all the high school dances and even won a jitterbug contest once. He was a good guy, a respectful guy. Just hello and goodnight kisses. I could live with that.

But three women, Aunt Caroline, Aunt Sarah, and my Mom, had other plans for me. Quietly and each in her way had set the stage for my choice, and thus, for the rest of my life. Here are their stories:

ᗡ AUNT CAROLINE – The Giver ᗡ

My Aunt Caroline wasn't really my aunt but was by marriage. Her third husband was my grandmother's cousin. Everyone felt sad for her since all four of her husbands had died fairly soon after the weddings. No one talked about that, perhaps because each husband had been richer than the one before and because Aunt Caroline was always paying tuition for any family member who wanted to go to college.

After my dad had graduated from Stanford, he got a job teaching high school math in Santa Barbara. After my mom had finished in Education at Phoenix Normal, she got a job teaching second grade in Santa Barbara. They met at a teachers' picnic, fell in love, and married.

As a wedding gift, Aunt Caroline offered to send them both to graduate school. They accepted. Dad got a PhD in math and physics at Cal Tech; Mom got an MS in Histology at Pomona. At graduation, I was in Mom's belly under her graduation gown, hidden so she wouldn't get expelled. It was 1932.

I still have her Dissertation: "The Effect of Cigarette Smoke on the Adrenals of Albino Rats," with slides.

I met Aunt Caroline when I was 7 or 8. We were visiting Dad's family in San Jose when an invitation came in the mail inviting me to join her for lunch in San Francisco. Gramma and Aunt Sarah were very excited. They took me shopping: they bought me a blue taffeta dress with a sash, black patent Mary Janes and matching purse, white gloves, lacy socks, and a white hat with flowers on it.

The day came. Gramma and Aunt Sarah drove me to the train station. They gave me over to the conductor, instructing him that I was to get off in San Francisco. Aunt Caroline's chauffeur was waiting for me there, looking very distinguished in his pale gray uniform and cap.

He drove us to the Fairmont Hotel in the very long car with a "child's seat" that opened up behind the driver's seat. We went way up the elevator to Aunt Caroline's apartment; he knocked on her door. I wasn't the least bit nervous since she and I had the same first name.

Aunt Caroline opened her door with a flourish and a smile. She had bright blue hair.

I froze but quickly recovered as she reached out for my hand and pulled me inside. It was gorgeous inside, and you could see all over San Francisco from her windows. We chatted for a bit, though I can't recall what we talked about.

Soon it was time to go down to the restaurant. At the table, I remembered to pull off my left glove first, then the right and lay them in my lap, then put my napkin on top. I followed along doing what Aunt Caroline did. First, we each dipped our fingers in a small bowl of water then dried them on tiny napkins. The waiter took them away and brought us each a bowl of ice with another bowl inside of it that had small shrimp hanging off around the sides. I don't remember the rest of the meal except for a dish of ice cream at the end. I mostly remember that we talked a lot and that a nice lady came to our table and told Aunt Caroline that she had noticed my good manners.

Several months later, back home in Flagstaff, a letter came from Aunt Caroline. I watched as Mom and Dad opened it. They just stood there and stared at it and then at each other, smiling. Inside was a check for my college tuition and a note that said it would be enough in 10 years if they would invest it wisely.

And they did. And it was.

When Aunt Caroline died, she left a piece of her jewelry to each of 12 women named Caroline.

☙ AUNT SARAH – Never Married ☙

My Aunt Sarah was my great-aunt, my grandmother's sister. She was the youngest of nine children and the tallest of them all. She wore a size 14 shoe. Maybe that's why she never married.

When her father, my great-grandfather, Doctor Benjamin Cory, wasn't tending to his patients, he was gambling or drinking or both. That's why my great-grandmother held day-school in the big house on 2nd Street. Aunt Sarah helped out. Maybe that's why she never married.

Aunt Sarah decided she needed to get a better education so she could better help out. In 1895, she went up the road to Stanford University, studied the language arts and graduated with honors. Some women students invited her into their sorority; she accepted. A man named Tom loved her, but her allegiance was to the school on 2nd Street, where she taught and supported the family, even after her mother died. Maybe that's why she never married.

Her sister, my grandmother, finally married at 39, had my dad when she was 40, and "fell weak." Aunt Sarah moved in to take care of everyone. Maybe that's why she never married.

When our family visited, Aunt Sarah took great pleasure in playing like she was my teacher. It was our secret game. It was Aunt Sarah who made sense of fractions for me. She said I was smart enough that I could go to college.

At 15, I brought up the subject of college and my tuition money from Aunt Caroline. Dad said college costs a lot more than just the tuition. He said he had only enough to send my brothers to college. He suggested I might better use Aunt Caroline's tuition money for my dowry, that girls didn't need college.

I told my Aunt Sarah. She offered this: if I pledged into her sorority, she would pay my "house bill," which was lodging and meals, but that I would have to make good grades and work for my personal money.

I accepted, and I did that. Aunt Sarah came to my graduation.

"Now," she said, "you will never have to depend on anybody, as you can take care of yourself. Whether you marry can be your choice."

Maybe that's why she never married.

∽ MY MOTHER – A Wise Woman ∽

When I was very young, Mother got down to my level, looked me in the eyes, and said solemnly:

"Be curious.
Question everything.
Trust your instincts."

Mom had wavy auburn hair and lots of freckles. From pictures I've seen of her with a trendy marguarette hairstyle, sitting in an early '20s Ford Model "T" Speedster with a custom speedster body, and another wearing a sheer, flowing wedding dress, she might have been a flapper or something rowdy like that.

But I experienced her as pensive, a good cook and homemaker. She was a loving wife and mother. She taught me how to do all kinds of things: cook, wash, iron, sweep, beat the rugs, and take care of my things. She taught me how to "BE" in the world with a remarkable litany of proverbs, like "You can't tell a book by its cover," "Don't cry over spilled milk," "A penny saved is a penny earned." More than a hundred of them.

I trusted her.

Even, or perhaps especially, on the day that she was leaning against the bathroom doorframe, watching me pick my pimples in the mirror.

"Sweetheart," she said, "I have to tell you the way it is." I turned, and we locked eyes. "You're not much to look at . . . and you never grew a chest, so if you want to catch a man, you need to be an excellent cook."

"Thank you, Mama." It was a huge relief knowing I didn't have to be pretty to get married, that there was another option, one I could do."

The next time we went to visit my Santa Barbara Gramma, I was on it. I tried to learn by writing things down while she cooked dinner. When she got a handful of something like flour, for instance, I would get her to put it in a measuring cup and then I'd record the amount on a pad. Many entries were in "handfuls," "half-a-handful," "pinches," "abouts," and ingredients like sheep's horn that don't exist anymore.

I guess this messed up her natural flow because the rolls didn't rise and the dinner didn't turn out right. She was upset with me, grumbling a string of Danish words that I happily didn't understand.

That wasn't going to work. No shortcuts. It became apparent that attending college to learn a lot about food and cooking was the next logical step in my life.

Aunt Caroline had given me tuition, Aunt Sarah had given me room and board, and now my mom got me ready for college. I'd need stylish clothes for Sorority Rush. Mom and I picked out dress patterns from Vogue, got the material, and she sewed for months. We were ready when it was time to go.

* * *

Yes, I made it! I pledged Kappa Kappa Gamma, Aunt Sarah's sorority. I was initiated March 3, 1951. The world had opened up its arms for me, and I jumped in.

HIGHER LEARNING

Chapter 9: Enlightenment

In 1950, social culture expected marriage. The challenge for the woman was to "catch" a husband who could support her, wouldn't hurt her, and she might even like. Our job was to be a homemaker and raise the children. Theirs was to support the family. We knew that falling in love could mess everything up. That "when a good relationship comes first, true love will follow." We were to stay calm and focused.

I picked the University of Arizona because it was only a 10-hour drive home; I had lived in Arizona, and it just felt right. The U of A was an established Land Grant College, so had an excellent Department of Agriculture, School of Home Economics, Department of Foods and Nutrition.

But the razzle-dazzle of my first days on campus threw me off balance, so much so that I thought maybe I didn't need to be a good cook. Within this wonderland of thousands of men and women my age seeking spouses, I just might get lucky right off. But not if I was in the School of Home Economics. No men in there.

I had an idea. I'd switch out a couple of my basic Home Ec classes for basic Ag classes where I could find a rich rancher to marry. I could spend the rest of my life riding horses. (I was 17.)

I did switch classes and got my new course syllabus with the outline and summary of topics to be covered first semester: Orientation, Composition, Chemistry, Botany, Agronomy, Dairy, and Physical Education.

It was a full schedule, but I was excited to be taking Botany, the nature of science and the life of plants; Agronomy, all about soil and farming practices; and Dairy, care of the cows and natural and industrial milk production. (Turns out I was the only female in the class and the only person who had never milked a cow.)

Sorority pledge life was busy with tasks and skills we had to accomplish before initiation: make good grades, community volunteer work, decorating the homecoming float, learning sorority history and songs, going to meetings, and looking good and being charming at social functions. We had dinner at the sorority house each night and a big meal on Sundays about 2 p.m. Sam was our old-school Southern cook: crispy fried chicken, buttermilk biscuits, hot buttered corn-on-the-cob, baked ham with sweet 'taters, gumbo, and red beans with rice. Delicious memories.

And there were school events: football games, basketball games, intramurals, and social gatherings.

But nothing enlightened me more than spending Thanksgiving at a dude ranch.

Chapter 10: The Dude Ranch

Just before Thanksgiving break, this nice boy in my Dairy class named Brian said his family had a "Working Dude Ranch" down in Wilcox that had three vacancies left for the holiday. "Since you're so green," he said, "I thought maybe you'd like to come on down." Green?

Two of my new dorm friends didn't have plans either, so we three decided to do it.

"Black Bart," a tall, lean, good-looking, 30-something cowboy dressed in all black picked us up at our dorm on a nippy Wednesday afternoon, and off we went, 80-some miles to the ranch. It was getting dark. We could barely see the main rustic log house as we drove up a long driveway. Smoke spiraling up from a rock fireplace chimney felt friendly.

Inside we met Brian's dad, the other guests, and six polite cowhands who seemed very excited to meet us. We had hot cider around the fireplace and chatted awhile. Then we learned about tomorrow's adventure: taking a long ride around the ranch, checking on the watering troughs and salt licks. We'd be back by 4 in the afternoon for a Thanksgiving Day feast.

Black Bart drove us to our tiny cabins, one for each of us, within walking distance from the main house. He showed us how to light the kerosene lamp and said there'd be a bell at 4:30 a.m. Breakfast was at 5 a.m. sharp.

When the bell rang, I jumped out of bed and into some warm clothes. I could smell bacon from the main house all the way to my cabin. A fire was going, and most everyone was there. Platters of pancakes, bowls of scrambled eggs, bacon, butter, syrup, and toast were already on the long wooden table. I slipped into an open spot on the bench. All was quiet as Brian's dad read a passage from the Bible. We said "Amen," and dug right in.

That's when Brian's mom came into the room with coffee. She was thin in a faded flower apron tied in the back that nearly swallowed her up. Her face was sallow, her eyes tired; her hair was pulled back with a rubber band. No one spoke to her. She didn't say anything. I tried to catch her eye, but she just poured coffee then quietly left.

Within 15 minutes, we were fed and on our way out to the animal stalls. "Doesn't your dad go with us?"

"No," said Brian. "He runs the business, and he reads a lot."

The cowhands saddled our horses and then theirs. Within 15 minutes we were off and riding into the dawn. It was a long day, just riding. A long day.

We came back, cleaned up, and went to the main house for the Thanksgiving festivities. The table was covered with two huge turkeys with dressing and some berry sauce, yeast rolls, string beans, and mashed potatoes with butter, apple cider, and pumpkin pies with whipped cream for dessert. Silently, we all sat down. Brian's dad read to us again. We said "Amen" and then ate this magnificent meal.

Later, I found out that there was a kitchen helper. But it was Brian's mom who did all the cooking and serving. I'd wanted to go to the kitchen to see if I could help out, but Brian said not to do that. His mom didn't want people in her kitchen, especially not the guests.

By 7:30 p.m., folks were filing off to their cabins. Tomorrow was a work day.

The bell rang at 4:30 a.m., and by 5, we were all eating again, this time, turkey hash with eggs sunny-side up.

We all went to the barn, but the cowboys were not saddling up the horses. Black Bart said, "Today we'll be castrating six to eight one-month-old calves." While silence fell on the guests, the cowhands were already getting things ready.

Buckets of soapy disinfectant water were at hand. A "calf table" was swabbed. We guests stood back and watched. Black Bart supervised the whole ordeal.

A calf was separated from his mother and laid on his side on the calf table. His front legs were tied. His back legs were held apart by two cowhands and tied down if he got too rambunctious. His scrotum was washed with the soapy disinfectant water.

A lady guest left when a cowhand leaned in with a shiny, sharp knife. He cut off the lower end of the calf's scrotum. The calf jerked and bellowed when cut and then again as the cowhand inserted his fingers up into the scrotum and carefully pulled the testes out. He put them in a bucket.

The calf was then taken to another room and placed carefully on a bed of straw. Black Bart said the bleeding would stop in a few hours. The calf would stay there until the incision healed, probably three or four weeks, that he would be treated with care and respect.

Eight calves later, they were done. It was noon already. Some of the guests went back to the house and napped or hung out in Brian's dad's big library. Some of us went out for a ride. When we got back, we wandered around outside the house.

There was a windmill, a hand pump, and a water trough out back. Two people working in the enormous vegetable garden waved; another nodded coming out of the chicken house with eggs. There were lots of pigs of all sizes in a pigpen with a lean-to pig house, and a slaughterhouse behind it.

All the food for Brian's family, the workers and guests was grown and processed right there. Brian said they usually would go into town on Saturdays, shop for general supplies and stay until evening for the big barn dance. Tomorrow we'd all go into town and have a good time, even the cowhands. But not his mom or dad.

Saturday morning was laundry time for everyone. There were enough clotheslines for two or three shifts. Since the sun always shone and the air was so dry, things dried fast. It was also cleaning day for the main house and cabins. Weeds were pulled, and slaughtering was done. About one o'clock in the afternoon, we had a light meal of potato salad and deviled eggs, with special meatballs for the guests. Later, we piled into cars and went into Wilcox.

Folks from all over came to town for the Saturday night dance. A big barn was decorated with hay bales and crepe paper streamers. A three-piece string band started playing around 7 p.m. Folks whooped and hollered, getting louder as the clock ticked on. It was stuffy and dusty, and though I wasn't in the mood to dance, I did anyhow. Black Bart didn't drink or dance. His job was to see that we had a good time and get us back safely. I was happy when we left around 9:30 p.m. My friends were tired, too.

After breakfast the next morning, Brian's dad held a short Sunday service. It was time to pack up and go home.

As Black Bart delivered us back to the dorm and helped us with our luggage, he asked if we had enjoyed our weekend.

Of course, we said, "Yes," and raved a bit.

"Did you enjoy your Mountain Oysters?"

I thought he was silly; there weren't any oysters on that dusty dry ranch.

"They were the special meatballs we had at lunch yesterday."

Blank faces.

"They were the testicles from the calves we castrated on Friday. They are a delicacy."

Silence. Looking at each other.

Um… I knew what I had to say. "Yes, they were delicious! Thank you for everything. I shall never forget you, the ranch, or Mountain Oysters."

We all had a good laugh.

Visions of that holiday rocked my mind for several days. Especially of Brian's mom. The real ranch life was a far cry from the one of my dreams. I better forget my fantasy ranch life and get serious. Think this thing through.

Did I want to be a good cook so I could catch a husband? Did I even want to get married?

I'd heard there was free Aptitude Testing for first-semester students, so I decided I should take it. I was dumbfounded by the results.

Chapter 11: Aptitude Test

Designed to determine a person's ability in a particular skill or field of knowledge

"Come in," said a deep, austere voice. I did. The man stood up from behind a large desk, solemnly extended his hand and asked why I was there and sat down. There was no chair for me. A placard on his desk said 'Counselor.'

"I'm a new freshman. I'd like to take the Aptitude Tests to be sure I'm on the right academic path."

Silence for a long minute.

"All right," he said flatly. "We don't usually give them to girls, but I do have a few open times."

Within a few minutes, it was all set up. I would come on afternoons for three days. The tests took a long time, but that was OK. In a week, I was called in to discuss the results.

This time, there was a chair for me. I sat respectfully as the counselor spread the test papers out across his desk and studied them. Back and forth went his head. Finally, he sat up tall, then leaned slightly forward and studied me.

"Well, Miss Hablutzel, it seems that you aren't particularly good at anything. Your scores are average across the board. But you don't have any low scores. That means that you would probably do fairly well in any profession you might enjoy."

Slight smile. Long silence. I just sat there saying nothing. Not good at anything?

He leaned back, crossed his hands over his big belly, looked me in the eyes, and said matter-of-factly, "Let me make a suggestion, Miss Hablutzel. Why don't you sign up for Home Economics spring semester? All the girls seem to like that."

There it was. Déjà vu.

The next week was Winter Break. I was glad for the time to be with family, lick my wound and regroup.

Home was the perfect cure. Good to hug family and hang out with friends. Vacation came and went with the usual tree, presents, dinner, and parties. I was anxious to get back to school. I wanted to get my life there on track. My future had been left dangling.

Turns out they had already slipped me right into the second semester of freshman Home Economics.

Chapter 12: College in 3 Nutshells
Academics, Jobs, and Skills

ACADEMICS

From the details that follow, the "takeaway" is this:

The field of Foods and Nutrition for human beings embraces a variety of subjects, approaches, and attitudes. Not conflicting, but merely differing sub-fields such as:

- Scientific inquiry into metabolism and related bodily functions
- Factors affecting nutrient value of food: processing, transportation, storage
- Soil health, organic vs. conventional food sources
- Food safety and pandemics
- Natural food vs. human-made, factory food
- Additives, labeling, toxins, and pesticides
- Infant and childhood nutrition, school lunch
- Home cooking, restaurant eating, meal planning
- Understanding traditional food practices within the US
- Popular diets, fads, media distortions, truth in advertising
- Effects of lifestyle practices

Students could select courses within these fields that best suited their interests. I chose practical and science-based courses as follows:

- Fundamental Biology – General Botany, Principles of Agronomy (Soils), Mammalian Physiology, Zoology, Bacteriology
- Foods – Food Study and Preparation, Meal Planning, Food Management, Consumer and the Market and Experimental Cookery
- Nutrition – Introduction to Nutrition, Advanced Nutrition, Readings in Nutrition, Laboratory Methods in Human Metabolism, Child Development and Nutrition Work with Children
- Dietetics – Diet Therapy, Institutional Food Management, Institutional Organization and Administration
- Chemistry – General Chemistry, Organic Chemistry for Students in Agriculture and Home Economics, Physiological Chemistry, Quantitative Analysis, Biochemistry, and Biochemistry Lab
- Math – Algebra, Trigonometry, and Plane Trigonometry

- <u>Supporting courses</u> – Economics, Family Economics, Home Management, Sociology, Psychology, Composition, Speech, and History

What I did was study like a dog. In time, I got the hang of studying.

In my junior and senior years, I was "selected" to oversee the sorority house Study Hall; my moniker was "The Bulldog." I'd come a long way since Mrs. Roseberry's first-grade class.

I graduated college "With Distinction."

JOBS – WORKING FOR MONEY

Counselors in the Department of Home Economics kept a list of jobs on campus that would support our goals. To work on campus, we had to be at least sophomores and have good grades. Following are a few jobs I took.

∾ Cafeteria Help ∾

Although a short order restaurant and a sweet shop were on campus, most everyone ate at the cafeteria (student headcount was 5,568). I started as a busgirl carrying heavy, clumsy trays of dirty dishes from the dining area to the washroom in the back. I lasted about a week. My grip slipped, sending the full load of dishes, glasses, and silverware onto the concrete floor with an explosive crash. Everyone looked.

They assigned me to the preparation room for salads. We workers sat on stools in front of a conveyer belt. For months, my job was to place a maraschino cherry carefully on top of the moving salads with the stem sticking up, or an olive, or some other decorative item. Later, I got to work the pie oven, like a pizza oven, with oven mitts and a long paddle, 24 pies at a time.

I observed the butchering of skinned and cleaned animals into traditional cuts, hamburger meat, and bones for soup. I watched the preparation of veggies for salads and steaming, and making vats of mashed potatoes, cake mix, or cookie dough.

Workers slipped in and out and around each other like dancers.

∾ The Sweet Shop ∾

Another semester, I worked in the sweet shop, making cones, malts, and banana splits. I was allowed to eat whatever I wanted (in the back room), and I did. It didn't take long before I got sick of eating sweets, but not of my job. It was fun.

↬ Lab Assistant ↫

My senior year, I worked in the research labs. Let me tell you a story about lycopene.

On a beautiful Saturday afternoon in 1953, I was in a basement laboratory in the Agriculture building, wishing I were somewhere else. Instead, I was a "student lab assistant" on a research project. This day, my job was to extract lycopene from tomato paste.

I set out a couple of beakers, a can of tomato paste and lit the Bunsen burner. I unscrewed the cap of a can of benzene, the solvent we used to extract the lycopene and set it down. To open the can of tomato paste, I clamped an old-style opener onto the upper edge of the can and then turned the side key to cut the can around the top edge. My wrist buckled, the tomato can slid sideways, knocking over the benzene. As I reached for a cloth to mop it up, my arm knocked over the Bunsen burner. A fireball instantly flared up, and a cloud of black smoke spread quickly. I ran for the door hollering for my boss. He ran in, smothered the flames, and suggested I go home to pull myself together. (I didn't get fired.)

Curious, I asked my boss about lycopene. Straight out, he told me that much of their research was to find components in food waste that could be easily and cheaply extracted. When we found them, we would conduct animal (mice) feeding studies to assess the nutritive or any other perceived value that might be marketable. Our current project was lycopene, as there was waste in the canned tomato industry.

It turns out that lycopene has antioxidant properties, so is sold as a supplement in today's market.

SKILLS - THE ABILITY TO DO SOMETHING WELL

A person never knows what skills one might pick up by just being around people and things they enjoy.

↬ The Rodeo ↫

Even though I was in the Department of Home Economics, I still liked to hang around with the Agriculture students, especially at competitive events like the rodeo.

There was a real quiet guy. Jack was not social at all, hung around

Caroline & Jack Team-Tying

Aggie Queen

the Aggies, too, off to one side, but always there. He rode his beautiful quarter horse in the singles events. One day, he had two horses in his trailer. He asked me if I'd like to ride.

"Yes," of course.

In Albuquerque, I had ridden horses as there was a public riding stable a bike's ride from my junior high school. I'd help groom and I rode horses that needed exercise. I took riding lessons on Saturdays, English and Western saddle.

That's when I learned that when you are starting to fall, go limp all over. It works. I've often fallen in my life and never broken a bone.

Several weeks later, Jack asked if I'd like to come to the university stables and work his horses with him. He had four gorgeous quarter horses. I went, and it soon became a weekend habit.

A few months ahead of the big rodeo, he asked if I'd like to learn to rope. He schooled me, showing me what to do. We practiced, and by rodeo time we were ready to enter the team-tying event. We took second place and became the talk of the rodeo crowd.

The following fall, I was elected "Aggie Queen." A full-page headshot of me in a cowboy hat is in the 1953 yearbook, and a copy now hangs on my wall.

∽ Song Leader ∽

Second semester sophomore year I moved from dorm living to the sorority house. There were 28 of us in 12 small rooms, two shared baths, and two sleeping porches, plus the rest of the house.

Everyone had duties. Fall of my junior year, I volunteered for Song Leader duty.

My youth had been filled with music. Like many

families in my time, we had a spinet piano in our house. We all took lessons, even Mom and Dad. Mom would bang out Tchaikovsky's Polonaise when she was frustrated. She'd play Beethoven's Moonlight Sonata when she was happy. After Dad had played Tchaikovsky's Piano Concerto No. 1 at his high school graduation, he swore he would never play again. Mom said he still had nightmares over his piano teacher whapping his knuckles with a conductor's baton if he made a mistake. But he gave in and started playing with the rest of us. Boogie-woogie. Said he'd be a barroom pianist when he retired.

All of us kids played an instrument or two at school. I played flute and piccolo in the band and orchestra; my brother John played sax and clarinet; Ben played the bassoon. In Shreveport, Dad installed a Klipsch music system and listened to classical music obsessively. I'd been in the choir at church and in high school and in Little Theater musicals. I took singing lessons, had a good range, but bombed at opera. Couldn't pronounce those words or roll my r's.

But, I had never been a "song leader." A conductor of sorts. It was a rough start: a raft of sheet music to learn and 27 girls to sing harmony. We practiced a lot.

We sang at dinner, on holidays, and went caroling at Christmas. Every Tuesday evening, we were serenaded by boys from a neighboring fraternity. We sang back to them.

Once a year, a fiercely competitive all-campus "Sing" was held in the outdoor amphitheater. My junior year, we sang "It Was Just One of Those Things," and we won first place my senior year with "Easter Parade." We even sang the "Messiah" together with a fraternity. We were good!

Chapter 13: Higher Woman Training

It was during the college years that I came out of abject ignorance and into plausible reality about women's issues. The culture of silence and judgment still reigned, but innuendos and shared experiences cut through the fog.

I learned about women's bodily functions, particularly the menstrual cycle. In the sorority house, the "alpha woman" would start her period, and within days, the rest would follow. We talked about the pre-menstrual feelings of desire and irritation. We talked about our aching breasts.

Those who had cramps would gather on the sleeping porch with warm lemonade, a couple aspirin, and a blanket.

Child Pose

Many of us would assume the chest-down, butt-up position that tipped the uterus so the blood could flow out smoothly. It is the "child pose" in yoga. We grumbled about the classes we were missing and would have to make up.

Conversations about how to handle aggressive male behavior were ongoing as such situations arose. How to protect oneself from physical and emotional harm were open discussions: "If a guy is hurting you, get away." "Always go on double dates or with groups." "Stay focused." "Don't drink or barely drink." "Steer clear of guys who had been drinking excessively." "Don't get in cars with guys you don't know well." "Be careful how you say 'No'."

Remember, there were no cell phones then, nor any way to reach out for help.

Yet, we were encouraged to enjoy social time with the guys.

Although we sorority girls bonded as a supportive group, there were subtle digs on occasion. Different reasons. Maybe jealousy, perhaps insecurity. Worth watching your back. Good practice for the real world.

On the academic side, I got a final slap down. I was doing so well with my studies and enjoying them so much, that I applied for a Graduate School Fellowship, as I would need financial assistance to continue my education.

"Well, sure, honey, you can apply for a fellowship, but you'd be wasting your time."

"Why? I have excellent grades."

"It's not about your grades, honey."

"What then?"

"Well, we only have three fellowships available, and we award them to the applicants who we think will benefit the most from them."

"I don't understand."

My graduate advisor paused. Then he told me the way it was: "You'll get married, raise a family and that'll waste our time and fellowship money."

Hum. He might be right. (This was the 50s.)

Deflated, I turned to go when he said brightly, "But your application to the program is welcome; we like girls here."

And then it was over. Last final exams. Graduation. Hugs and tears. Time to say goodbye.

Professional Years

Chapter 14: Human Nutrition Research – USDA

The counselor's office at school had a list of available jobs for graduating seniors to consider. Five jobs were on the list. Two were for dietetic interns. No, I didn't want to work in a hospital filling doctor's orders. One was with General Electric doing in-store demonstrations of how to use their kitchen appliances. Not my style. Another was teaching nutrition at the University of Maine. Intriguing. The last was working with a government research project to determine the least amount of food people needed to eat to maintain basic health.

BINGO! There it was. Human Nutrition Research. My future profession.

The Home Ec Department Head, Mrs. Thompson, gave me a letter of recommendation; I mailed it in with the application form. By graduation, I had an acceptance letter with details.

The letter told me to report right after Labor Day to the Human Nutrition Research Laboratories in Beltsville, Maryland, 30 miles north of downtown Washington, DC. It said I would be assigned to one of many teams who would conduct "human feeding studies" at private locations.

I packed up two medium-sized suitcases and a mini sound system that Dad made for me: a two-foot-tall triangular wood box with a speaker, woofer, and tweeter inside, a stylish turntable with three sapphire needles, and a half-dozen platters: Shahrazad, Beethoven's 6th, and some Broadway musicals.

Platter: An LP; a long-playing phonograph record designed to be played at 33.3 revolutions per minute

Dad drove me to DC and helped me set up in the downtown YWCA where I could stay for two weeks. We drove to the research center where I found out I could take the Greyhound from downtown DC to a bus stop in Beltsville, where a shuttle bus would take me on out to the "farm" (a collection of USDA research buildings). Work was from 8 to 5.

At Orientation, I learned that the Knoxville project began in mid-October, so the kind folks at the YWCA suggested I stay at the famous—and cheap—McLean Gardens until then. I took their advice. Interesting place: once a lavish estate, it was torn down in 1942 and rebuilt as a garden-style dormitory complex to house government defense workers during WWII. After the war, the rooms were rented out to locals. Residents had small rooms and shared bathrooms. A big, bright cafeteria offered healthy food and the grounds were gorgeous. On weekends, I toured the Smithsonian, art museums, and the Library of Congress.

USDA Minimum Daily Requirements

The Human Nutrition Branch of the USDA MDR (Minimum Daily Requirements) project was designed to quantify the amount of food and nutrients needed to stave off illness based on the hypothesis that the difference between what goes in and what comes out is what humans need.

The history of the USDA's nutrition research, advice, and guidelines goes back to 1894. They have been continually updated over time, adopting new scientific findings and new public health marketing techniques. Interest spiked in 1941 with the onset of WWII and the challenge of finding the best way to feed the troops. The Quartermaster Corp teamed up with the USDA to provide the most nutritious K-Rations possible.

During that time, it became apparent that no one knew the nutritional needs of the fighting troops, much less of the population in general.

After the war, various medical, nutrition, and research groups took on the challenge of addressing the issue. The USDA Human Nutrition Research Branch studied several primary population groups and identified the results as the MDR, Minimum Daily Requirements.

These data were subsequently combined with other research findings and re-termed the RDA, Recommended Dietary Allowances, the levels of intake of essential nutrients that, on the basis of scientific knowledge, are judged by the Food and Nutrition Board to be adequate to meet the known nutrient needs of practically all healthy persons.

The RDAs are still being used today with yearly updates.

For the research project, test subjects by gender and age categories lived in closed locations for six weeks. I was assigned to work with eight eight-year-old girls in a house in Knoxville, Tennessee, converted for the project. The girls lived as normal a life as possible; however, a project staff person or parent was always with them to intercept that cookie or take an off-site urine sample. The girls ate and slept at the group house.

The project staff lived there as well, helping out with house chores, homework, games, story time, and performing various medical tasks. Mine was collecting blood each morning via the dreaded finger stick.

All the meals for the project had been prepared in the Beltsville kitchens and frozen ahead of time from foods gathered from known locations throughout the country and tested for nutrient content. Half the meals were frozen and held at Beltsville, and the other half were kept in freezers at the testing locations. On-site, meals were thawed, warmed, and served as prescribed. Uneaten portions were collected for analysis from each child for each meal and snack, as were urine and feces. These waste products were collected in containers beneath a long, short wooden outhouse-looking contraption with eight holes across the sitting area. Each girl had her own hole.

Of course, everyone understood that many variables were involved in this project. Some variables didn't show up until we were in process, like determining the nutrient content of some of the foodstuffs.

For that, we used the Proximate Analysis procedure to determine the amount of moisture, ash, protein, fat, and carbohydrate (which was calculated from the total) of each food. Minerals and vitamins were analyzed from the ash. But first, samples had to be prepared for analysis. I helped with this during those six weeks before we left for Knoxville.

First, the foods were dried under infrared lamps in an air oven to determine the moisture content. Samples were handled with tongs and when dry, were placed in individual airtight jars from Germany. The lid of the jar was shaped like a mushroom with a stem that was slightly tapered down. This stem fit snugly into the neck opening of the jar due to chemical etching of the juxtaposed surfaces. The etched surfaces had to be lightly greased so they would gently slip as the top was twisted down into the neck of the jar or else they would bond so tightly the jar would never, ever open.

During this time, I learned from experience that the nutrient composition of foods is a function not only of the food itself but the soil, climate, and location of its source. For example, lettuce from fields in New Jersey, Texas, and California had very different nutrient compositions, even when they were the same kind of lettuce. It was finally decided to lump the data together for each food and calculate an average.

Food Composition Tables cannot tell us the exact amount of nutrient that is in a particular food. That's not possible. The number in the table is an average, an approximation.

Upon returning to the farm after Knoxville, I was assigned the task of analyzing samples from our project for sodium, potassium, and calcium content, in triplicate, all day, every day. I worked by myself in a tiny room using a spectrophotometer and writing down the results in ink on a tablet.

Typical Analytical Tools – 1955

Spectrograph

Spectrograph

A spectrograph separates light by wavelength and records intensity using a multi-channel detector. Each food has its own spectrogram depending on its variety, growing conditions, type of soil, and other variables. Note that I recorded the data by hand into a notebook. I was alone in a tiny room, doors closed, no air flow allowed.

Analytical Balance

Analytical Balance

The analytical balance measures a very small quantity of material. The material is carefully tapped into a vial that is placed on a pan inside an enclosure. The doors close tightly so dust does not collect and so any air currents in the room do not affect the operation of the balance. The sample must be room temperature to prevent natural convection forming air currents inside the enclosure, causing an error in reading.

Paper Chromatography

Paper Chromatography

Paper chromatography is a technique for separating dissolved chemical substances by taking advantage of their different rates of migration across sheets of solvent-impregnated litmus paper. A precise drop of test solution is controlled by the diameter of the delivery tube and the careful release of pressure by the chemist's tongue on the other end, as shown.

If results varied too much, I had to repeat the test.

Envision the uniform for the Dept. of Agriculture's women in research (top two pics) as being drab cornflower blue, ill-shaped, and reaching mid-calf. No class. The men wore white lab coats. (The lab coat I'm wearing in the bottom pic was from when I worked at Fisheries a few years later.)

When the six weeks was over, and we returned to Beltsville, another chemist, Betty, and I got an apartment together near the farm. She had a car, so I didn't even have to take the bus. We shared the cooking, so I learned some new recipes.

But her Midwest hometown boyfriend missed her so much that he moved close by. When they got married, I moved, too, and my life exploded with joy!

My supervisor had suggested I might like Georgetown, an area on the west side of DC. She and her sister had lived there many years. It was a long way from the farm, but she offered to give me a ride. I looked in the paper for apartments, houses to share, and roommates wanted. I found two and went to check them out. One was a no-go. The other was perfect. A two-story historic home on 34th Street, just up from N Street, a few blocks from the Potomac, and a couple of blocks from Georgetown U.

But more importantly, it turned out that Georgetown was a small, but lively, social neighborhood inhabited by young professionals. Yahoo!

Four young women were looking for one more and they liked that I was a government researcher. Serious Evelyn, the oldest (about 34) was a statistician; I don't remember where she worked. Bubbly Winkie worked on the Hill for Senator Strom Thurmond. Grad student Lisa was a lawyer with the Internal Revenue Service, and Beverly, just out of school like me, was a fresh, new cartographer for National Geographic. They all had genuine, welcoming smiles. I moved in toot sweet.

Evelyn was the manager, collected our rent, paid our bills, and was a liaison with the owner. Bedrooms were upstairs, and each girl took care of her own. We had one shared bathroom. Downstairs household duties switched each week. Two girls shared cooking and kitchen duties. The cook was responsible for the week's dinner menus. She bought and cooked the food and cleaned up with her helper. Breakfast was a la carte. The helper had to keep the kitchen tidy.

Everyone got to be the cook. On my turn, I introduced the girls to slow-cooked pork shoulder with potatoes and onions cooked in the drippings with a side of Danish slaw. They liked my Holiday Ham best, oven-baked with canned pineapple slices affixed to the top with cloves and sprinkled with brown sugar that caramelized during baking. We each tried to show off our culinary skills, and all ate cheerfully if dinner bombed.

Friday nights, we could invite a friend for dinner. Saturdays nights were party night all over Georgetown. Here's how that worked: People who hosted parties just cranked up some music and opened their front doors. Usually, five or six parties were going on at the same time in the neighborhood. (That was a different time, folks; hard to imagine it's happening in today's culture.)

Not only did I experience a variety of meals in my new home but I surely learned about hors-d'oeuvres on Saturday nights.

You know how it is when you meet someone: "Hello, nice to meet you, what do you do?" I always introduced myself as a nutritionist (more inviting than 'research scientist'). Chatting with a fellow one evening, he asked, "Do you eat sunflower seed pancakes? I hear they are healthy. What do you think?"

Sunflower seed pancakes? (Very off-the-wall weird in those days.)

There it was, another lesson: that there were apparently many things I didn't know. College, work, and even my life were just stepping stones in my nutrition education.

* * *

After a time, I met David. We got to know each other on long walks in Rock Creek Park. He had lived in DC all his life and had good friends. David's dad was with the Federal Bureau of Investigation, and his mom was an interior decorator with Woodward and Lothrop, painting watercolor renderings; she sang opera beautifully, though not

professionally. David was a quiet, pensive kind of guy, studying literature at George Washington University and writing short stories for fun. We were compatible with similar goals in life. With my high school best friend as my maid of honor, we married on August 15, 1956, in Shreveport, Louisiana, where my parents still lived, at the historic Episcopal Church. We honeymooned in New Orleans.

Back in DC, we moved to a tiny house in a subdivision, Connecticut Avenue Estates, in Silver Spring, north of town. Happily, a carpool to the farm was available. Getting places was a determining factor in deciding where one would live, as important as price.

We bought a mattress, a folding card table with four chairs, a Goodwill sofa, and the complete 30-book set of the Encyclopedia Americana that came with its own bookcase. Information was hard to find if you didn't live near a library.

We got a dachshund, named him Fritz. The three of us went hiking most weekends, usually on the Appalachian Trail, going into the trail around Harper's Ferry in West Virginia, not too far from home. We'd hike all day Saturday, spend the night at a Civilian Conservation Corps shelter, and come back the next day. Vivid colors, shadows, the sweet smell of fresh air, the light crunching of twigs underfoot, Fritz stalking hidden prey. We rarely encountered other hikers. Peaceful.

I cooked a lot, honed my skills. What fun preparing meals from my past: pot roasts, fried chicken, cheese dishes, baking bread, pies, making hand-churned ice cream. I had Mom's and Gramma's recipe books, *Betty Crocker's Picture Cookbook*, 1st edition 1950, that I gave to myself after college, and *Joy of Cooking*, 1943 edition. (I still have these same books and use them regularly.) I even fixed David's favorite recipes from his mother and from *The Gourmet Cookbook I*, circa 1950, which his mother gave us.

Newly married couple cooking was in fashion. We would get together with three of David's high school buddies and their new wives on a rotating weekly schedule, each couple taking a turn at cooking the meal. Each couple tried to out-cook the others. David really got into it and was crowned the "King of Hollandaise."

We tried to settle into this comfortable routine, but such a life was not to be.

Chapter 15: Fishery Products
FISH AND WILDLIFE SERVICE

I saw in the Federal Register that a GS-7 chemist job was coming up in the US Bureau of Commercial Fisheries Technology Laboratory on the University of Maryland campus in College Park, not too far. I was just one chemistry course shy of qualifying, so I quickly enrolled at George Washington U night school in downtown DC and signed up for "Proteins and Amino Acids," a course I could use. When it ended, the job was still open. I applied and got the job and a nice raise. I put a deposit down on a VW Bug. Goodbye tedious job, goodbye drab uniform.

Hugo W. Nilson was a tough boss. No matter how early one might come to work, Hugo was already there, standing at the parking-lot door with his pocket watch in hand. He clocked us in.

If you were even one second late, you got docked an hour's pay, but you better not leave, just scoot on in and get to work.

Our building had grass and trees all around with windows on every side. We had offices and labs upstairs and down, a big room for animal-feeding studies, and a library where we met for coffee on our 15-minute breaks at 10 a.m. and 2:30 p.m. and our one-hour lunch.

We were an 18-person research team: the boss (Hugo), three project leaders, four chemists, four animal husbandmen, four home economists, a statistician, and a secretary.

Right away, I was assigned to the Quality Standards team to establish freshness and safety parameters for shellfish, food fish, and processed seafood products. Research in the laboratory focused on the technology required to maintain freshness of shrimp, blue crab, oysters, haddock, and cod held during simulated commercial refrigeration.

In the field, team members spent time in commercial processing plants to better understand the real-world conditions that affect quality. We all participated in all phases of the research.

My first field trip was a month at a shrimp processing plant in Brunswick, Georgia. Shrimp were taken from the boat to a "grader" that separated the shrimp by size, then to a huge table where they were shelled and rinsed, and on to the kitchen where they were made into retail products like shrimp creole, then to the packaging room and right into the freezer.

On another field trip, I worked in a haddock and cod processing plant in Boothbay Harbor, Maine, where the fish went from the boat onto tables on the dock. There, skilled workers boned them lickety-split with long, thin, sharp knives, rinsed and put the fillets on a conveyer belt going indoors to a "shaper" for either fish sticks or fillets, onto the breading rooms, the packaging room, and into the freezer. Scraps went into soups.

The upbeat ambiance of a blue crab packing plant on Maryland's Eastern Shore made light of being away from home. Cotton-clad middle-aged women, called "pickers," worked at long tables, so fast their fingers seemed to fly. Chatting continuously, they could pick the white lump, regular, and claw meat separately without ever looking down. They sounded like birds chirping. They raced to fill as many containers as possible in a day, as they were paid by output. Containers were picked up frequently, chilled, and delivered to retail stores right away.

During my time at Fisheries, I picked up two evening teaching jobs in downtown DC.

The first job, American Cooking, was an Adult Education class held in the high school Home Economics kitchen. There were ten students, speaking mostly Spanish. I only remember two things about the class. First, the food allowance to buy the necessary groceries was skimpy. The second is of the last class of the semester. The students wanted to bring the food so they could show me what they ate at home. Each brought a delicious dish. What a feast! We ate heartily that night.

The other class was Basic Nutrition, an elective at the George Washington University Medical School, rumored to be a 'crib course.' Eight young men showed up. Three sat in the front of the class with pencils in hand. Five sat in the back of the room, side talking. The first day, a student in the back raised his hand and asked, "If it's true that you are what you eat, then why doesn't my head have a head on it?" Chuckle, chuckle. And so it went until the end. My final exam was a simple, high-school-level question: Describe and discuss the digestion, absorption, and utilization of food in the human body. Three students passed; five didn't.

* * *

One morning, Hugo wasn't at the door. The night before, he had died. Boom. Just like that. A massive heart attack and he was gone, only in his early 50s.

Project leader Donald Snyder, a fresh PhD and barely 30, just took over. Right then and there. Said to me, "You're my assistant. Move your stuff into my office." Seamlessly, we kept everything moving along. The lab's research projects never skipped a beat. The next fall President Eisenhower honored both Donald and me with the Distinguished Service Award. I was 27.

Around this time in history, there was an abundance of fish in the oceans. So much that only the choicest were taken to market leaving "trash fish" behind; over 5 million tons a year were tossed back into the water. Visionaries saw ways to use trash fish for fertilizer, animal food, and even "to feed the starving world." The Food and Agriculture Organization launched a global effort to address this issue, and our lab was called up to participate.

First, methods were developed to extract the oil and water from menhaden, an abundant trash fish in the North Atlantic, leaving protein and bone, then ground into a powder. A little gritty and a little smelly, but it's what we had. It was termed FPC (fish protein concentrate) and re-termed fish flour when being considered for human consumption.

Our lab's role was to find ways to incorporate FPC into the diets of poultry and hogs to their benefit and to determine the feasibility of using fish flour in the diets of humans. Our animal husbandman, Robert, handled the hog-feeding studies; poultry scientist, Larry, conducted the chick-feeding studies; and I did rat-feeding studies to zero in on factors affecting variations in nutritive value and to test for antimetabolites.

Data on the growth of three groups of young rats were compared: the control group which was fed a standard lab-rat diet, a group whose diets had added fresh menhaden, and the third group with added menhaden FPC. I loved doing this project, even though free weekends were now history as rats eat and poo every day.

The rats got excited at feeding time: fresh mash, supplements by syringe and their favorite, lettuce. Daily, I weighed them, measured their 24-hour food intake, gave them fresh food and supplements, and cleaned their cages.

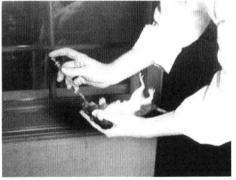

I submitted a request to the Bureau asking them to sponsor me to continue research into the nutritive value of fish flour so I could meet the requirements for a Master's degree. They agreed. And I submitted a request to my sorority, Kappa Kappa Gamma, for a graduate fellowship, which they gave me.

I was deep into it now!

The project, "Determination of the Protein Content and Quality of Fish Flour," was designed to take about two years, the amount of time I would need to complete the required coursework:

1957–1958 (two semesters): Recent Advances in Foods and Nutrition, Problems in Nutrition, Readings in Nutrition, Advanced Biochemistry 1 in the fall and 2 in the spring, plus Nutrition for Community Service and Seminar

1958–1959 (two semesters): Advanced Biochemistry 3 in the fall and 4 in the spring, Protein and Amino Acids, Audio-Visual Education, Research (both semesters), Intro to Agricultural Biometrics

After many rats and severe late-night studying, I finished the thesis: 74 no-error pages with two carbon copies, typed with my trusty old Underwood, including 16 photographed tables of data and graphs. What is that like?

How to Type a 2- Carbon Document in the Late '50s

You take a piece of white typing paper and put a carbon sheet behind it, and then another piece of white paper with a carbon behind it, and finally another white paper. Carbons are tissue-like papers with black carbon dust on one side. So, you are making an original and two carbon copies with each key strike. (If you're not careful, the carbon gets onto your fingers and smudges everything you touch, including your just typed pages).

You stack the pages correctly, put them all together behind the roller, and carefully roll them in so the pages line up and don't slip on one another. Then you roll the roller to the point where the text begins. Key in the letters of the words and make spaces with the space bar. The keys strike an ink-impregnated ribbon that moves along between two spools, one on each side of the typewriter, as you key in each letter. The roller moves at the same time. When a bell rings, you are near the edge of the roller and must finish or hyphenate the word, then smoothly run the roller back to the right with a handle attached to the roller on the left side. The paper moves down one line as it reaches the right side. Then, type in that next line.

There is a tab key and also a shift key for making capitals.

If you make a mistake, you have to start over. You cannot erase the original nor the carbon copies. Correcting a mistake may only entail typing that one page over unless the correction affects previous pages. Major changes early in the document often require typing everything all over again. Whiteout had not yet been invented, and even if it had, it would not have been permitted.

The graphs and tables were meticulously drawn by hand with drafting tools, photographed, and reduced to the prescribed sizes. They were then pasted onto the appropriate pages in line with the typed letters.

All this while, David had been studying diligently hoping to finish college and get on with life. As an elective, he took a course in Philosophy and so loved it that he switched his major. His professor suggested that he go on to graduate school to study Philosophy at a deeper level, so David submitted a dozen applications.

I had just scheduled the defense of my dissertation when another of life's unexpected events changed my life, again. David was accepted into graduate school at Harvard . . . in Cambridge, Massachusetts.

Chapter 16: Food and Flavor Research

ARTHUR D. LITTLE, INC.

∽ Food and Flavor Laboratory ∽

We packed up our stuff and moved to Cambridge with excitement and trepidation. We found a large and convenient apartment on Rindge Avenue, across from a library, and a bike ride to the campus. With the help of my Human Nutrition and Fish & Wildlife colleagues, I landed a job with Arthur D. Little, Inc, just a mile away.

ADL was a well-known and highly respected "Research for Hire" company, everything from engineering to food. Projects in the Food and Flavor Division ranged from product development to solving food-related problems for industry, schools, and the military, and yes, even countries.

My first day on the job was a happy portent of things to come. The Food and Flavor Lab was bright with sunny windows and crispy-clean research facilities including a test kitchen. As I stepped inside, a busy bunch of younger-than-I-expected lab techs welcomed me with warm handshakes. My new boss, L.B. (Johnny) Sjostrom, a smiling Swede, was equally welcoming and obviously well-liked.

I got a locker and a lab coat and sat right down to observe the first flavor testing of the day. It was the Flavor Profile Method of Flavor Analysis.

Six lab techs took seats around a round, white laminated table upon which six bananas, evaluation forms, pencils, table knives and napkins lay in orderly fashion. At the sign of the leader, the techs peeled their bananas, then sniffed, sliced, and sniffed again, tasted, very slowly chewed, and swallowed. All the while, techs wrote on their forms. No one talked.

When all were ready, discussion began.

After much practice, I became a panel member, participating in creating flavor and aroma profiles for companies that made puff pastries, chocolate candy, soda, chips, diet foods, butter substitute, mouthwash, toothpaste, deodorant, perfume, and my favorite, dog food. (I worked with 28 research dogs who did the actual tasting.)

The Flavor Profile Method of Flavor Analysis

The Flavor Profile Method of Flavor Analysis was developed by J.F. Caul in 1957 and published in Advances in Food Research 7 5. It is considered the "mother" of many other descriptive methods for flavor analysis. It was perfected by scientists at Arthur D. Little in the late 1940's and has been used extensively over the years, and is still in use today.

The description herein was lifted from my paper, The Flavor-Modifying Effects of Disodium Inosinate, published in the *Journal of Food Technology*, 18 9 (1964) with my permission.

The flavor profile method (Caul, 1957) is an analytical tool used for describing flavor-modifying properties. This method relies on a highly trained panel of tasters. Panel members analyze the total flavor complex of a product by examining, separately, the aroma, the flavor-by-mouth, and the aftertaste of the product.

The overall sensory impressions (i.e., amplitudes) imparted by the aroma and flavor-by-mouth (including flavor residues after swallowing) are recorded as either low, moderate, or high.

Individual sensations obtained, called "character notes," are assigned descriptive terms. These may be the names of components of the food product or may be associative words. In the aroma, the sensations obtained are due to volatile materials. In the mouth, they are due to basic taste stimulation, aromatic materials, and feeling factors.

In addition to the defined qualitative components of the flavor complex, intensity values are assigned to indicate quantitative relations. An additional parameter for measurement involves the relation in time of the sensations perceived. This ordered series, called "order-of-appearance," completes the profile compilation.

A tabulation of the flavor sensations remaining in the mouth several minutes after swallowing is called "aftertaste."

The compilation of characteristics – qualitatively, quantitatively, and in time sequence – for the aroma and the flavor-by-mouth is called a flavor profile. A composite of flavor profile data from 5-6 panel members provides the working tool for flavor evaluation.

---

* * *

Boston was overflowing with rich history, music, theater, restaurants, and the Appalachian Trail was just a few hours away. And now with my 8-to-5 job and David's school schedule, we were able to get in some "culture," fresh air, and exercise. We often took the trail up into the White Mountains. It was a magical time.

○ Fish Flour Formula ○

During the '50s, the Food and Agriculture Organization of the United Nations had devoted time, money, and energy to the study of the world's fishery resources and how best to exploit and use them. For the most part, this focused on animal food as we had done at Fish and Wildlife. But eyes were turning to human consumption. ADL was already onboard designing mini fish flour processing plants to be located in Nigeria to address the food crisis there.

ADL put me to work developing an infant formula using fish flour, soy powder, dry milk powder, and sorghum, abundant in Nigeria.

Words cannot describe what a mess that was. The fish flour was dry, granular, and not water-soluble. The soy powder was fine, dusty, and not water-soluble. The dry milk powder was dry, granular, and only slightly soluble. These ingredients were to be shipped to Nigeria in sacks, where the locals would mix them with water and sorghum and feed the mixture to their babies via a bottle.

No matter how creative I got, the ingredients glommed up and wouldn't pass through the nipple of a bottle—not even when I diluted it a lot and used a wide-holed nipple designed to pass porridge. Ultimately, we dropped the bottle idea and created a gruel to feed to the babies. It tasted nasty and smelled of fish.

Years later, I learned that the babies wouldn't eat it. When "forced" upon them, they would scream for hours. It turns out that knowledge about soy was in its infancy and folks didn't realize that soy contains ingredients that a sensitive digestive system cannot tolerate. Soy can cause stomach pain, cramping, bloating, gas, and diarrhea.

Meanwhile, even though my Master's thesis research had just been completed and not yet published, I was invited to present my research at the FAO Fish in Nutrition International Congress in Washington DC in September 1961. My colleagues warned me NOT to express my opinion, which was that fish flour would never make it in the market due to its pervasive fishy taste and smell. They said it wasn't my place to say. What did I know about other markets? Like starving children to feed.

This warning was a valuable lesson: A scientist is to present only the results of the experiment and may judge only whether the results answered the question being tested. Period. A "universal" interpretation is not their prerogative.

Though my heart was pounding, the experience of being onstage presenting to researchers from many countries, each with a headset to hear what I had to say via an interpreter, was amazing. Abstracts of the presentations were published the following year in an imposing book entitled *Fish in Nutrition*.

✑ My MSG Story ✑

It was a huge feather in my cap when Johnny Sjostrom, Director of the Food and Flavor Lab, appointed me to be the Project Leader of a research study for Merck Chemical Company. The chemists at Merck had created a pure form of monosodium glutamate, MSG, a key ingredient in soy sauce. They also created pure forms of two similar compounds, "cousins" of MSG. Merck wondered whether these chemicals would enhance the flavor of foods, and if so, which foods and how.

I was proud and honored to have been chosen to lead this research, as I was a woman and not yet 30. It was the early '60s, when women had not yet broken that glass ceiling and youth was rarely respected.

Yes, I was breaking the mold and relishing the role. A project leader worked with a team of bright scientists, and in this case, they were mostly wives of Harvard and MIT graduate students. I had an office and even secretarial assistance. I sported a Jacqueline Kennedy look and wore my hair in a French Roll. I got to write and present progress reports to Merck's Product Development team at the company headquarters in Rahway, New Jersey, on a regular basis.

Life was good.

The chemicals we studied were three similar nucleotides: MSG, disodium inosinate (IMP), and disodium guanylate (GMP).

They looked like rectangular salt crystals under the microscope, varying slightly. They all tingled on the tip of the tongue and had a mild salivating effect. Each had its unique physical and taste characteristics.

Our job was to evaluate these chemicals as flavor enhancers, substances that improve or deepen the flavor of foods without changing their natural flavor. You know what I mean if you have used salt, butter, Worcestershire sauce, or a squeeze of lemon with your foods. All have "blending" properties.

The home economists in our test kitchen incorporated varying amounts of each of these chemicals into prepared soups, meat, fishery products, dairy products, cereal and grain products, vegetables, tomato products, and a variety of diverse foods.

Our taste-test panel described the aroma, flavor-by-mouth, and aftertaste of these foods using the Flavor Profile Method of Flavor Analysis.

Each of these nucleotides gave specific, yet similar results in their enhancement properties. MSG did a good job, though GMP was more mellow but expensive to produce. IMP was the strongest and most versatile, showing promise for use in meat products, soup, and some vegetables as well as inducing a "meaty" taste and increased viscosity.

In the end, Merck decided to go with MSG, probably because it was the most cost-effective.

MSG has been a big player in the flavor enhancement market because it makes processed foods taste better. That's important to the industry since the processing of food usually removes the primary flavor components of the original natural foods like the aromatics and fats.

Our research was a two-year project and an excellent piece of work. It was published in *Food Technology*[1]. I'm very proud of it.

* * *

That fall, I noticed that I was pregnant. Not in the plan, but exciting nonetheless. After all, I was pushing 30, the last age that it was deemed medically safe for a first pregnancy. I kept quiet until my belly began to push out my lab coat. The boss didn't say, "Congratulations," or anything like that. He just said he personally would take over the MSG project, which was close to completion, and then asked me to organize the data to date and sketch a potential paper for publication.

I had to resign within two months. So much for nudging the glass ceiling.

The real-life consequences of this eluded me until I got restrictions: I wasn't allowed to use the elevator (I might trip getting in or out), nor stand very long. I was to hold the handrail when using stairs. I was to be out of sight when visitors came. I couldn't participate on the flavor panels. I had to stay in my office and "finish up."

---

[1] Kurtzman, C.H. and L.B. Sjostrom, The Flavor-Modifying Properties of Monosodium Inosinate. *Food Technology*, 18, 9 (1964)

The idle weeks ahead gave me a welcome rest. A chance to get ready for childbirth. For a new life. I decorated the small bedroom with blue checkered curtains and pasted animal cut-outs on the walls. It was evident to me that he would be a boy, as he had plummeted my insides relentlessly with sharp heels, and I was so huge I had to hold up my belly with a long Indian scarf tied up and around my back and shoulders.

We chose Harvard Medical School Clinic, as they offered a financial incentive for students and their wives who would allow the event to be a "hands-on" experience for the med students. I broke water on a Friday night. We went to the hospital. On Saturday, a handful of excited students showed up with several doctors. They were thrilled to learn that the baby was breech. I wasn't. The doctor got to demonstrate how they go up and manually turn it around so that it will come out head first.

Labor took a long time to get going in earnest, as I didn't dilate enough. At last, the baby entered the canal, and in spite of my effort, he got stuck. (Maybe because I was a 110-pound woman with small hips?) The doctors had noted earlier that I had an inwardly-tilted tailbone but had thought that it wouldn't be a problem. But he was a BIG baby. It was too late for a cesarean, as by then he was well into the canal. After discussing the pros and cons of this situation with the students, and without saying a word to me, the doctor unceremoniously snapped my tailbone to open the passage. (I will never forget that sound. Yes, I was drugged, but awake for all of this.)

It was late now, and all were getting tired. The students cheered me on, "You can do it!" "Breathe" They coaxed me to let go and release the yet unseen baby. Way past midnight, and into pre-dawn, I gave my best last push and out he came. Cheers went up all around. The students congratulated the doctors and themselves on a job well-done. They congratulated me on the birth of my baby girl. GIRL? Yes, a big red-faced girl. They held her upside down by the feet to drain, smacked her butt to start her breathing, cut the cord, washed her up, wrapped her in a blanket and handed her to me. It was now 7:10 a.m. on Sunday morning.

After sufficient drugs to keep me pain-free and awake for more than 48 hours, I slept like a drunk. After I woke, the nurse brought the baby to me, but nothing happened; the baby wouldn't wake up to nurse. So the nurse gave me "nursing lessons." Through the next day and the next, no colostrum, no milk. The doctors decided that there was something wrong with me and gave my baby a bottle of cow's milk; didn't ask, just told me. She vomited it up. So they gave her soy milk, the new, high-tech miracle of the year; didn't ask, just told me. She held it down, so we were both released from the hospital.

I've read similar child-birthing stories from those years. Many women speculate that both mother and baby were drugged unnecessarily during the process.

David's mother came up from DC to lend a hand. What a blessing. For several weeks I lay on my side in bed, bathing the stitches from the episiotomy with ice-cold witch hazel. (Episiotomy: a vaginal incision to make the delivery more comfortable with less pain than tearing.) Soon, I began sitting on a donut pillow.

New Gramma cooked and fussed with the baby and quietly took down the blue checkered curtains and sewed up new ones with an English pastoral print in pastel green on a deep cream background. With sheep and Bo-Peep.

Through friends at work, I found a young mother with two daughters, ages 2 and 4, who was delighted to take baby Beth at two months. ADL had a job opening, though not as a project leader; I was just glad to get a good lab job again.

∽ Metrecal ∽

Mead Johnson had been making supplements for infants and invalids for years, but in 1959, it launched a weight-loss product for adults. It came as a powder containing powdered skim milk, soybean flour, and corn oil, and was fortified with vitamins and minerals. Customers were to mix it with water. They called it "vile, disgusting," etc.

We tried to fix it, but that didn't work very well. We just couldn't make it taste good.

So they asked us to create a more acceptable product for their Metrecal line. We came up with a concentrated, 300-calorie, high protein soup in a four-ounce can that tasted like real beef-vegetable soup that could be taken to work if desired. I was assigned to the team.

That one didn't sell well. Soon, Meade Johnson gave up on Metrecal.

∽ Strawberry Soda ∽

Working in the Food and Flavor Lab teased my curiosity about how everyday foods were made industrially. The strawberry soda project gave me true light-bulb moments.

ADL housed a vast and fascinating, worldwide collection of pure elixirs and distillates of natural plants in a spotless flavor library equipped with the latest scientific equipment imaginable. When a project came asking us to create strawberry soda, we were on it!

We examined the strawberry elixirs and tinctures we had on hand to determine the primary components of "strawberry" aromatics. Strawberry aromatics are what you smell when you smell strawberries: the thousands of tiny, lightweight molecules that are released by the berry. Picture an invisible fog of microscopic particles dancing in space, more intensely near the strawberry, thinning as it travels away from the berry, possibly reaching into a far area.

Aromatics are a class of organic compounds, many of which emit odors, the primary source of flavor. We smell them before eating the food, and then, again as we eat. They travel up the channel from the back of our mouth into the nose, stimulating the "smell" receptors there.

To identify the strawberry aromatics, we had to separate the aromatic molecules in strawberries from one another so we could identify and quantify them individually. We accomplished this using an exciting new analytical procedure called gas chromatography, which works like this: The sample is placed in a flask in a water bath that is subjected to slowly rising temperature. Because of their varying weights and structures, the aromatic chemicals in the sample are released at different temperatures, the lighter, more volatile ones being released first. They rise through a tall glass column. At the top, the column takes a side turn into a downward slanting condensation coil. The aromatics form droplets that fall into test tubes set into a moving circular tray below.

In order, the contents of each test tube are analyzed and plotted on a graph.

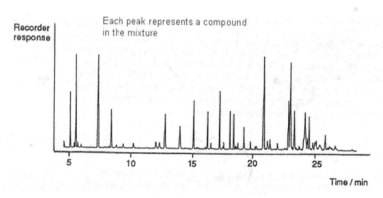

Many peaks and spikes were displayed on our strawberry graph, but only a few tall peaks, meaning there were only a few aromatics in sufficient quantity that our chemists could analyze and identify them.

"What about all those smaller peaks?" I asked. "Aren't they part of the strawberry flavor?"

"Well, probably, but we don't know what they are, and we don't need them to make the soda. We only need to know the chemical composition of a couple of the aromatics that had the tallest peaks. That's all our brains need," the project supervisor explained. "They will recognize the prominent aromatics and 'fill in the blanks' by association with something they already know, like real strawberries. It's easy to trick the brain."

He went on to note, "If the predominant aromatics aren't available commercially, our lab chemists will create them or substitute something similar."

As I looked at all those unknown peaks on the graph, it struck me that we humans don't know most of what's in our foods, or what's missing in processed food.

Consider this, too. The year was 1962. I'll bet that with today's technology, we could find many thousands of components in strawberries that we haven't identified yet, or may never.

And what does it mean to trick the brain? Does our brain "fill in the blanks?"

Did we trick the brain into thinking it was getting real strawberries? Can we *actually* fool our brain into thinking we are getting authentic food? How does the rest of our body respond to that? The body parts that need actual nutrients?

Does it matter? What if some of those components are nutrients that are essential for our state of wellness? Yes, it matters.

That poses an even broader question. Fast forward to 2016 for the moment:

Key Lime Pie

It was birthday time, and none of us had time to bake a cake, but the birthday girl loved key lime pie, so we stopped at Publix and bought one, put some candles on it and had birthday pie. Tasted pretty good. It was gelatin/pudding-like with a tangy lime flavor, a thin graham-cracker-like crust, and decorated with whipped cream rosettes and a twisted slice of lime.

A few of us old-timers noted that it didn't taste like the ones we made in the good-old-days. I compared ingredients:

Traditional Key Lime Pie

Graham cracker crumbs, unsalted butter, sugar, sweetened condensed milk, egg yolks, key lime juice, key lime rind, heavy cream, salt

Publix Key Lime Pie

Dairy blend (milk, sugar, whey, nonfat milk, magnesium hydroxide, sodium citrate) lime juice (water lime juice concentrate, key lime juice concentrate, lime oil, sodium benzoate), enriched unbleached flour (wheat flour, niacin, reduced iron, thiamine mononitrate, riboflavin, folic acid), milk, sugar, partially hydrogenated soy &/or cottonseed & palm kernel oil, water, graham flour, vegetable oil (soybean, palm & palm kernel oil, TBHQ for freshness), heavy cream (cream, milk, carrageenan, mono-diglycerides, polysorbate 80), high fructose corn syrup, corn syrup, hydrogenated coconut oil, salt, brown sugar, acacia gum, malt syrup (malted barley, corn), soy lecithin, molasses, carbohydrate gum, polysorbate 60, polyglycerol esters of fatty acids, leavening (baking soda, sodium acid pyrophosphate, monocalcium phosphate), cornstarch, natural & artificial flavor, malt extract, sodium citrate, disodium phosphate, xanthan gum, sodium bicarbonate, caramel color, beta-carotene, vanillin (artificial flavor), yellow 5 & 6. May be garnished with toasted almonds and lime slice.

Questions kept nagging at me:

If persons eating key lime pie from Publix had never eaten traditional key lime pie, would their brains just accept the Publix pie as being the real deal? Will a time come when every new food, every imitation food, every processed food becomes the real deal?

Does using the traditional name imply that a product contains old-school traditional ingredients? Even when it is on the label of a product containing none of the original ingredients?

* * *

I was riding high with my work, feeling worthy even without my short-lived project leader title. At the same time, I was getting tired and frustrated. I wanted to be at work, and I wanted to be home with my baby.

That dilemma seemed small in October of 1962 when a terrified world held its breath for 13 days, seemingly on the brink of nuclear war. David rented a TV so we could watch the Cuban Missile Crisis unfold, minute by excruciating minute. We packed our VW with camping equipment, blankets, food for ourselves and 6-month old Beth, ready to go. Cities were a dangerous place to be during a nuclear war. We knew of some caves up in the mountains.

Though a peaceful resolution finally took place, the scare stayed with us, as it did with most everyone, in a peculiar way. The world was tense, wary, and introspective.

Winter was coming on. We hunkered down, David preparing his dissertation and studying for his Master's finals in February and me calming down and counting my blessings. February came, and then March, and then it happened. He got the results. David didn't make it; he was not invited into the doctoral program.

Chapter 17: Stepping Back

Our choices came down to one: apply for a doctoral program elsewhere. The University of Maryland accepted him. Good news. Like going back "home." The Fish and Wildlife Service had an opening coming up at my old lab for a desk job reviewing incoming project proposals. I could assist in the analytical chemistry lab in the meantime.

Nice to be with old friends again.

We found a sweet little house only 11 miles from the campus in charming Old Greenbelt, one of three "green" towns planned in 1935 in the New Deal era as an "ideal" self-sufficient cooperative community.

Folks at a local church suggested I contact a recently divorced mother looking for a playmate for her young daughter who was born deaf. Our meeting was quite surprising. Within minutes, 18-month-old Beth and 2-year-old Kristen were laughing and crawling around together on the floor, as Beth couldn't stand or walk.

Beth had been born with a club foot, and it was time to see a specialist. They put her in a cast from toe to knee; that was to be replaced every six weeks with a straighter one, slowly coercing her foot and ankle into normal alignment. A rubber disk protruded from the bottom so she could stand and learn to walk. It was Kristen who got Beth to use it. Soon they were running around together.

∽ Automated Biochemistry ∽

Techs in the analytical chemistry lab were developing ways to automate the manual work of performing the actual tests for documenting spoilage breakdown in fish and shellfish. The lab benches were covered with Rube Goldberg-looking contraptions of pulsating motors, yards and yards of tubing and joiners, and custom glass containers. Aliquats of the test solutions and reagents were mixed in the process of being pushed through this quagmire, quantified, and results were printed on graph paper.

This hands-on automation work was familiar to chemists of the day and was the forerunner of fully automated systems currently in use.

↬ Essence of Science ↫

Soon the desk job became available, a change of pace.

I took over the task of reviewing project proposals from individuals wanting to do their own research. We had a budget for that. The projects receiving funds had to be well-designed and free of bias.

We required that the proposals include the six basic steps of research design:

Observation: I could sell more chickens if they would grow faster.

Question: Would they grow faster if I added fish meal to their diet?

Hypothesis: I could find out by measuring the weight gain of groups of chicks fed different amounts of added fish meal in their diets during a specified time, like six weeks.

Method: Here the applicant would detail his/her plan to test this hypothesis.

Experiment: Data had to be collected, tabulated, and analyzed using standard statistical procedures. We would assist the citizen-researcher with this.

Conclusion: Did the data answer the question? If not, how could the hypothesis be modified to get a conclusive answer?

We required a copy of the results of his/her experiment.

This job gave me a deeper understanding of the intricacies of observation, research design, statistics, and interpretation of data. It has helped me judge the quality and claims of both genuine and popular "science."

An add-on benefit was that I came across the little tongue-in-cheek book *How to Lie with Statistics* by Darrell Huff and illustrated by Irving Geis, first published in 1954. It gave us a lot of laughs.

> *It's still a best seller after all these years and is even more appropriate in today's world. It's the Spin Doctor's Bible on how to manipulate people's minds with numbers and the Advertiser's Guide to selling us stuff. It is also a handbook for folks trying to get to the truth about goods and services. See Appendix 7 - Reliable Resources*

↔ Crash and Burn ↔

Things were not going very well at home. David had been drifting into a different person for some time: sullen, moody, fidgety, explosive, and now started staying out late studying at the library. One morning he was not there, had not come home at all. No husband, no car.

The teen daughter across the street had her well-used Karmann Ghia sitting in the yard with a For Sale sign on it. I knocked on their door and asked if I could give it a test drive, to work and back. She gave me her keys. Same thing that night and the next day. (Remember, we didn't have cell phones in those days.) No way to find him, except to call the police, hospitals, and the Philosophy Department at school, which I did. They had no news for me. After the third day, I bought the Karmann Ghia.

Beth and I soldiered on. Close to Christmas, he knocked on the door, said he was OK now, and hoped he was welcome back. Shortly after the holiday was over, he disappeared again. About Valentine's Day, I realized I was pregnant.

Kristen's mom and the troops at work were supportive in every way.

What a blessing to be a Federal Government employee at this moment in time. Due to their non-discrimination policy, I was allowed to work until the contractions came. My co-worker, Mary, drove me to the hospital on September 16. The delivery was smooth; within minutes after wiggling out of the womb, being smacked on her butt, and gulping some air, Beth's little sister had a smile on her face. I watched the whole thing via mirrors all around. It was a glorious moment.

Upon awakening the next morning, still in the hospital, I heard a familiar voice say, "I'm here to take you and Beth and our new baby home." I didn't want to open my eyes.

"Home" it turned out was a house he had rented in Athens, Ohio, where he had gotten on as an Instructor at Ohio University. David had finished his PhD and was now "ready to support his family." He gave me money to hire movers.

I struggled with overwhelming indecision—whether to "do the right thing," keep the family together and go, though I didn't trust him or even really like him much anymore. I would have to leave the professional life I had crafted over the years and that I loved.

Or should I stay, nurture my profession, and be a separated, single parent? At that time, 1965, divorce was not an option as the state of Maryland only granted divorces initiated by women if she could show proof of extreme abuse or a photo of her husband in copulation with another person. Nor could I close our joint checking account or open my own.

My head ached relentlessly, and I couldn't sleep. Trying to think of the girls. What would be best for them? David could easily get custody of the girls if I tried to divorce him, even if I had the required photo. That surely would not be to their benefit.

I got too much advice from my friends. Thoughts, fears. Running together. Dreams intertwining, night and day. Not hungry. I finally called my mom; she told me to keep the family together, that in our society, life as a single parent, divorced or not, would be a worse Hell.

I trusted her.

I called in the movers, said goodbye to my friends and to my professional life, gathered up the girls and the dog and headed west to Ohio.

Transitional Years

Chapter 18: Demise of the Good Wife

Athens was a small town of about 6,500, not much there besides the University of Ohio. Finding my new home was easy enough with the town's map I picked up at a gas station. David was expecting us. The movers had come and gone. I'd made up my mind to be a happy mother, homemaker, and a good wife.

I set up the kitchen, got out my cookbooks, and cooked three times a day. I even fixed baby Anne's food from scratch, not trusting Gerber or Beechnut, knowing from having worked at Arthur D. Little that their products were mostly modified starch with just a percent or two of actual vegetables. One day I wrote a letter to Beechnut complaining. They wrote back thanking me for my interest in their products with a complimentary case of 12 jars of the same food I had complained about.

I sewed matching pinafores, sundresses, and play clothes for the girls with the Featherweight Singer Portable Electric Sewing Machine 221-1 my folks gave me for my high school graduation present, never used. David made them a sandbox out back and a rabbit cage for the thankless bunny we got them for Easter.

Walking with the girls to the grocery store and the park were our main adventures. At the park, I met two mothers who had once been preschool teachers. One had a large rec room in her basement. We got our heads together, furnished the rec room with a child-sized work table, and brought books and toys from home. I made and posted flyers, and put an article in the local paper. Soon, there were a dozen kids. Our project morphed into the Hocking Valley Play School.

That's all I remember about Ohio except that David had to put in a lot of evenings at school with seminars and counseling students. Happily, he got a better teaching job at the University of Florida in Gainesville, a lively town of about 100,000. With his better position, we might have more family time there.

We drove to Gainesville in June to find and secure a place to live. We found a classic old home in the historic district of Gainesville about 10 blocks from the Philosophy Department on campus, biking distance. An elementary school was only a few blocks away. Perfect.

The girls and I drove back to Athens to pack up and hire movers. David would move into the new house, greet the movers, and get things set up. The girls and I would come along as soon as possible.

We cruised into Gainesville late in the afternoon after a two-day trip. I had no trouble finding our house. I parked, jumped out of the car, sashayed onto the porch, opened the door, and went in hollering, "David, we're here."

"Daddy, we're here."

No response. No sound. Boxes. Unopened.

"Where's Daddy?"

"I don't know, honey. But he'll be along soon. Let's look around."

The welcoming foyer had a high ceiling with a staircase leading to the second floor. Double-pocket doors on each side of the entrance led to a large living room on the left and a large dining room on the right. Both rooms had floor-to-ceiling windows and fireplaces. An ornate chandelier hung low in the dining room. French doors that opened to a library and guest bathroom were at the far end of the living room. A large, old-fashioned kitchen and pantry were behind the dining room. I opened the fridge. Empty and warm. I turned on the faucet. No water.

We went upstairs and poked around: four bedrooms with big closets and a bathroom with a footed tub; no shower. I pulled the toilet chain. No flush. Two beds had been set up with mattresses. Movers usually did that. With some daylight left, we unpacked the car. We found and ate the sandwiches and soda left from the trip. Then we lay down on the beds and fell asleep exhausted.

Early the next morning with the girls still sleeping, I slipped out to find food for breakfast. The next-door neighbor was out getting her paper.

"Hi," I said.

We introduced ourselves.

I asked about David.

She hadn't seen anyone at the house.

I asked her if I could use her garden hose to rinse off the kids. Of course. As soon as they woke up, we pulled her hose into the old barn behind our house, and all three of us rubbed ourselves clean.

Soon after we'd had breakfast, here came David.

"Hi. Saw the car. Didn't know you'd be here so soon," not looking at me.

"It's all right," I lied.

David was all smiles now, hugging and kissing the girls.

"I'll get the electric and water hooked up today. Here," he said handing me a utility knife. "You can get started unpacking these boxes." He turned and started for the door.

"You aren't going to help?"

He grinned back at me, "I have a job," and walked out the door.

Women hid their disappointments, frustration, or anger in those days. No point in starting a losing battle.

The water and electric came on the next day, but we didn't see David until three days later. Meanwhile, the kids and I took long walks around the neighborhood, the duck pond, the park, the library. Wondering. The only thing I could do. We had no house phone yet, but even if we did, it was highly inappropriate for wives to call or bother their husbands at work, the only place I knew he might be.

When he finally came, I whispered, "David, what's going on?"

"What do you mean, what's going on?'

"David, the girls and I have been here for four days, and you haven't been here hardly at all."

"Something's come up."

"And?"

He raised his voice, "I said, something's come up."

"David, that's not good enough. What something?" Silence. "We've made plans; we have a life together. We are husband and wife . . . with children."

"Plans change."

"David, I need you to tell me what's going on."

His face darkened, slowly stepping in, eyes connecting, cold, measured. "You don't need me for anything. You never have. You don't need anybody. You are just fine all by yourself. You can handle anything."

Déjà vu. I remember hearing these same words before. From him. He had given the money he earned as a teaching assistant to a student of his

THE BITE OF HISTORY

who had a baby and no job or something like that. I'd stashed that memory long ago.

"A colleague, David? A student? Someone you just met needs you?"

Abruptly, he turned and left. He always walked out, I realized.

☙ The Angry Wife ❧

I fell into righteous anger by evening. What the Hell! I'd spent the last ten years of my life supporting him so we could get to this place in life, and he dumps me? Boom. Just like that. I fed him, nourished him, encouraged him, saw him through thick and thin, and he leaves me? I ironed his damned oxford cloth shirts for years, seven a week. No wrinkles.

Did David ever thank me for ironing his shirts? Not that I remember. After all, it's woman's work. Expected. What a self-centered, insensitive ass. Cruel to the children and me. What more could I have done? What more would anyone else have done?

Slipping now into self-blame, sinking into the sofa, I heard my culture: "It's a woman's job to make the marriage work." "Behind every successful man is a good woman." "A woman's place is in the home." Had I been too demanding? Had I expected too much from him? What was I doing wrong?

☙ The Retrospective Wife ❧

Long-squelched hurts bubbled up.

When we had moved back to Maryland after Harvard, David had been sullen, acting differently, lying—claiming he was at the library long after I knew they had closed.

I was pretty sure he was having an affair—like the time he didn't come home and I had to borrow the neighbor's car to get to work.

And the night the phone rang at 3 in the morning. David wasn't there; I answered thinking he might be in trouble. A female voice said, "Is David there?"

"No."

"Well, do you know where he is?"

"No."

"Do you think he might be with Lisa?"

"I wouldn't know." Click

How to iron a button-down oxford cloth shirt

Oxford cloth is a traditional shirting fabric, particularly for more casual styles of dress shirts. It is durable and naturally resistant but not impervious to wrinkles. Back in the day, they were 100% cotton. Polyester was yet to be invented. Thus, they needed to be ironed slowly and carefully so as to dry during ironing, but not scorch.

First, you wash them in warm water with extra scrubbing inside the collar and cuffs, shake them out, and hang them to dry by putting the top edge of the shoulder/sleeve seam on the clothesline with two clothespins.

While they are drying, make starch. In a pot, blend a couple of tablespoons of cornstarch in a small amount of water until it dissolves. Add about 4 cups of water and bring to a boil very slowly, constantly stirring until it fully thickens. Dilute this until it is the proper consistency for oxford cloth.

When shirts are barely dry, bring them in and lay them flat. Take one and place it on a table or countertop. Hand-smooth it open. Starch it by dipping your hand into the starch pot, shaking it out a bit and then cupping your hand over the shirt, fingers up, shake it lightly, so the starch water comes through your fingers in perfect droplets. (Takes practice.) With the other hand, turn the shirt this way and that, so every inch gets a drop or two of starch water. Then roll that shirt up, not too tightly, about 1 foot wide, laying the roll on a big towel.

Do each shirt this way and add each to the big towel. Now, roll them together in the towel, folding in the ends, and put it in the refrigerator overnight. Next day, take out one shirt and iron it. And so on until they are all done.

To iron a shirt, first clean the bottom of the iron: Put a piece of blank newsprint down on the ironing board, sprinkle with salt and run the iron back and forth till the iron is clean. Then heat the iron to the "cotton setting" with an electric iron. If you are using a wood stove, put the iron face down on a hot burner plate just long enough to get a light sizzle when you tap a wet finger to the bottom of the iron. You'll have to repeat this often, as the iron cools fairly quickly.

Now, iron all the parts of the shirt that have double layers of cloth: the inside of the double seams that hold the front buttons and buttonholes. Then lay out the yoke onto the ironing board, outside down, inside up. Hold it so you can use the tip of the iron to press the inside seams at the yolk/sleeve. That done, lightly press the entire inside of the yolk. Now, do the insides of both cuffs. Then iron the inside of the collar, giving extra pressure to the back side of the buttonholes.

Now the sleeves. If you have a sleeve board, use it. (This is a small ironing board you place on top of the main ironing board and is sized to fit inside a shirt sleeve.) Otherwise, set one sleeve out long-ways on the ironing board. Press the outside of the cuffs first. Then lay the sleeve so that the long bottom seam from armpit to cuff faces you. Holding it, hand-press the sleeve upwards and long-ways until there are no double folds that would cause a wrinkle. Hold that in place as you now move the iron along the bottom seam pressing upward almost to the top, but stop an eighth of an inch from the top so that you do not make a crease. Flip it over and do the other side. Then the other sleeve, same way.

Now put the top shoulder seam of one sleeve over the tip of the ironing board and press both shoulder and sleeve together until flat. Do the other side. Then iron the outside of the back of the yolk.

Then the collar. This is tricky. Lay the outside of the collar long-ways on the ironing board. Hand-stretch it first, pulling on the front corners until the seams relax. Then push the whole collar out flat using your palms. Now iron from the center back to one corner, then from the center to the other corner. Then iron the full collar, using the tip of the iron around each buttonhole. With both hands grab the end sides of the collar and pull wide holding until the seams loosen up.

On to the main body of the shirt. Iron the back first using long even strokes from neck to bottom. Press the mid-back pleat open to avoid making a crease. At the top next to the yoke, lightly press about a quarter of an inch of the crease so that it will stay relatively flat. Now, press each of the front sides, top to bottom. Go slowly and evenly over the double seam with the buttons and buttonholes.

Take the shirt off the ironing board, hold it by the shoulders, and shake it. Put it on a hanger. Button the collar and front. Then hold the top of the button front panel and pull it down firmly, then do the same for the buttonhole front. That loosens the threads to avoid puckering.

After some practice, you should be able to iron an oxford cloth shirt in half an hour.

For years, David insinuated I was unfaithful, that I was sleeping with guys when I went to professional meetings. Or when I got a vaginal yeast infection: "At it again, huh? Who is it this time?" Interesting slip; he was the only one I'd been with. "I saw how you and the butcher looked at each other. Can't even trust you to go shopping." Jealousy haunted him.

I suggested we see a marriage counselor. "OK," he said, "but not together."

I found a counselor whom I saw only once. Two minutes into the session he asked, "How's sex with your husband?"

After prudish me had recovered, I responded. "OK, I guess. I do what I'm supposed to do, but I don't like it if that's what you mean."

"Why not?"

"Because he's not very nice about it and it hurts."

"Tell me what it's like."

"Well, when he wants it, he comes into bed and tells me to get ready; I put in jelly. He puts his penis in me and pumps back and forth until he comes, gets off, and goes to sleep. I clean up."

"What hurts?"

"His penis is too big. It doesn't fit all the way in, so he pushes too hard."

"Do you have orgasms?"

"I don't think so."

"Have you ever talked to anyone about this?"

"Of course not."

"What did you think intercourse would be like?"

"Everyone said that girls will find out on their wedding night and that it will be wonderful."

The counselor was quiet for a moment then in a soft, kind voice said, "Many women have had a similar experience as yours. Women have little or no knowledge of sexual intercourse when they marry. Neither do men. Most men learned about sex in the locker room or from girly magazines. Most men have no idea how to bring a woman to orgasm, or even that they have orgasms. I suggest that you talk with your husband about this. Don't be afraid. Find a way that the two of you can both enjoy sex together. It is natural and will take your marriage to a happier, healthier level."

"How'd it go with your counselor?" I asked David.

"Fine."

"What did you talk about?"

"I just told him the truth, that you aren't spontaneous." That threw me. I wanted to tell him about my session with my counselor, but he kept talking. "He said for me to remember that I am the man. That I have every right to satisfy myself, to do what I need to do for me."

"He said that?"

"Yes, and he's a priest." Dead end.

∽ The Confused Wife ∽

My self-pity shifted as I thought of other possibilities. Maybe I just don't like sex, that blaming David is my excuse. Maybe I am just not feminine, that I have messed up hormones. A freak of nature. Yes, I am cold. Insensitive. Even when he gave me marijuana and said it would make sex better, it didn't.

Or maybe I'm scared of sex because of what happened when I was very young.

AGE 3 – The Yardman

One day, the old yardman across the street motioned me to come over. He talked funny, but I could tell he was asking if I wanted to see the baby kittens in the attic of the barn. Mom had told me always to be nice to him because he was mentally disabled. He went up first to steady the ladder for me, and as I got to the top, he spit on his fingers and slid his hand up my leg and his fingers into my panties. He smiled real big.

I was confused. I remembered when my Mom had gotten mad at me the time I lifted my dress to show off the ringworm on my tummy. But the yardman didn't exactly lift my dress, so I was nice to him, but then I got a funny feeling when he wiggled his fingers up in my private place. It wasn't like tickling; it made me have to pee. So I scooted down the ladder and went home. I knew if I told Mom, she'd be mad at me, so I didn't.

AGE 5 – The Babysitter

Mom and Dad would go out sometimes, and when they did, they hired Wayne, the high school boy who lived behind us, to babysit. I liked him; he laughed a lot and played games with me. Sometimes his friend

Jim came, too. They were both on the baseball team at school. Wayne even showed me the scabs on his chest where the ball had hit him.

One night, after my brother John and I had gone to bed, they both came into the bedroom. Wayne woke me up and whispered, "We're going to play a game in the dark. Be real quiet, so we don't wake up John." John slept on the top bunk. Wayne pulled down my covers and got up on top of me with one knee on each side. I was trying to figure out the game when he pushed something soft but hard up until it touched my private place. I tried to tell him he was hurting me, but he put his hand over my mouth and pushed harder.

I couldn't breathe. Stars swirled in my head. I couldn't think. I could only feel the hurt. After what seemed like forever, he suddenly got off of me in a huff. "Here, Jim, you're small. You try, I can't get it in."

"No, I just can't do it."

"Come on!"

"No, I don't want to." They left the room, arguing.

Shaking and cold, scared and confused, I covered myself. Wayne came back in and stood by my bed. He looked down at me hard. "If you tell your folks about this, I'll kill you."

I lay there. In a fog. In pain. Wondering why Wayne wanted to hurt me. I thought he liked me. My heart hurt. He didn't have to threaten to kill me. Never would I ever tell anyone. My Mom would be mad at me. I knew it would hurt her. I couldn't think what Dad might do.

* * *

Having been fondled and sexually attacked so long ago might have been related to my present problem. Hard to know. However, it was clear to me that trust has a dark side.

I do know that I feared the hateful look in David's eyes when I questioned him, opposed him, or even sometimes when I just tried to talk with him. "Can't we just talk about it, David?"

"No, there's nothing to talk about."

"It's about my feelings, my love for you, my heart."

"Cut the theatrics, Caroline. How can I talk with you? You don't even know the rules of logical discourse." He was like that with his friends and classmates, too, especially at Harvard. It's called "one-upmanship." (Dictionary Definition – a way of *behaving* in which someone *tries* to get an advantage by appearing to be more *skillful, important,* etc. than others). He loved it, wouldn't quit 'til he had won.

Whenever he turned red-faced with anger, screaming in my face, my stomach dropped, my heart raced, I sweated, I had to poop.

Or, it could be that his constant put-downs had worn me down. "It's a simple question." "Don't you know anything?" "No, you can't go with me to the party. Your lack of social skills embarrasses me." "You can't talk about anything interesting, just stupid things like food." "Of course, you're illiterate; you never read."

Seems silly, but the worst put-down was when we sat down for meals. Meals I had made to please him. From the grocery store to our table. He'd bring a book to the table and read while we ate, and on Sundays, he set the whole paper up between us so we couldn't even see each other. He grew angry if I interrupted his reading. I doubt whether he even knew what he was eating. Basically, I ate alone.

Now, here on the sofa, I was delirious with legions of memories that spilled forth, memories carefully stashed away. I felt helpless, worthless. I cried well into the night. I had been a total failure at marriage, unable to keep a husband happy. Just didn't have it in me. I thought of committing suicide. At the time, suicide seemed rational.

But if I did that, David would raise the girls. The bastard. I couldn't do that to them. I went next door and asked the neighbor to watch the girls. I told her I might be having an appendicitis attack and asked for directions to a hospital.

When I got there, I asked to see the psychiatrist on duty. His nametag said *Dr. Zorch, Psychiatry Resident.* A young man. He listened.

After a while, I calmed down. Dr. Zorch suggested I go home and get some sleep. He gave me a vial of sleeping pills and his number to call if the anxiety came back. I did call, several times over the next week. I couldn't let it go. I'd given up my beloved professional life to follow my husband because it was the right thing to do. 'Til death do us part.

And so, there I sat alone in my living room, a stranger in a new town, no job, kids to feed, living on my savings, and no desire nor energy left to deal with an arduous husband.

* * *

"I just saw Daddy," said Beth running into the house. "He told me to tell you he was coming over tonight at seven o'clock to read me a story."

"Where did you see him?"

"Out front. Driving by. I met Mary."

Stunned again, but I was not surprised.

Beth picked out her favorite book for David to read and was in her pajamas at seven o'clock waiting. No David. 7:15, no David. 7:30, "Where's Daddy?"

"I don't know, sweetheart. I'll read to you until he gets here."

"Oh, no. It has to be Daddy."

"Why?"

She looked down and whispered, "Because, Daddy says you can't read right."

There it was. The last straw. The breaking point. He never showed up; Beth sobbed. I made a life-changing decision.

∽ The Rebellious Wife ∽

The next day we walked to the library, Beth pushing Anne in the stroller. We registered for a library card. Beth got some books and I got a newspaper. Back home, while Beth read her books and Anne napped, I read the paper. A meeting was coming up for Parents without Partners. I went.

The room was full, at least 40 people, three of them men. A friendly lady shared her story, asked me mine. I told her I was looking for someone to share my big house. She said that a secretary in her office at the hospital was looking to move closer to town with her kids. On her lunch break, the very next day, Janet rang my doorbell.

Saturday, she came back with her kids. The lineup went like this: Scott, age 7; Beth, age 4; Tod, age 4; Dana, 2 and a half; and Anne, 18 months. They got along well together. Janet and I sketched out a plan that assigned one of us to a week's duty of watching the kids and meal prep with clean-up. The other person was "off duty" that week. Soon, Janet and her kids moved in, and our new lives began that beautiful summer of 1966.

I can't remember how I learned about teaching jobs at the brand new Santa Fe Junior College. I put in an application and got a cool job teaching Introduction to Science. I was allowed to make my own syllabus. I unpacked the clothes I had worn when attending meetings or making presentations to clients. The Jackie Kennedy look was still in style and still fit. With a bit of polish, my two-inch heels looked fresh. Wearing stylish clothes lifted my spirits.

As we were both working girls, Janet and I got the younger kids into daycare; Scott was in elementary.

Janet was all about having a good time. "You need to meet people," she said. We invited friends over on Saturday nights when the kids were with their dads. Her friends from the University of Florida and mine from Santa Fe. The living room, entry hall, and dining room opened into one big room. We moved the furniture back, turned on dance music, and here came our friends bringing food and drink, an upbeat attitude. We closed up at midnight. Someone always stayed to help clean up.

Word got around. In time, we had lists of names of people who wanted to come to our parties. We could accommodate 60 people. Everyone was respectful. Neighbors had been warned and invited to attend.

The morning after, we'd meet up with friends and head to the Ichetucknee River for a day of tubing (riding down the river in big inner tubes), or to one of the many springs to snorkel or to picnic somewhere.

My best therapy was the late evenings when Janet and I sat at the kitchen table, discussing life. We talked about food, healthy meals, fashion, the double standard dealt to women, raising kids, how our parents raised us, the drug culture, music, divorce.

"I know why your guy is like he is," she said.

"Yeah, why?"

"Because you're smarter than he is and he can't stand it. That's why he puts you down all the time."

"I don't know; he's pretty smart."

"Maybe, but you were successful while he was flunking Harvard."

"Well," I responded, "I know why your guy is a loser."

"Yeah, why?"

"Because every time you fall, you bounce back smiling, and he can't stand it."

"You think so?"

"Sure."

At the library, I learned that only six months of residency was required to file for divorce. Women could file. I stewed in anger, now deciding that David had not kept his end of our agreement, society's expectations. He was not supporting his family nor apparently had he ever intended to do so. I retained an attorney.

My next memory is of David and me in the attorney's office discussing details. He advised us that Florida is a community-property state based on laws passed to protect women. Our case was unusual, as it "protected" David. I was the one who worked and supported the family. I had savings, made the down payment on our house, and invested in an orange grove in Arizona. None of that mattered. Half of everything was his. I took the orange grove and David took the house, which was fine with me; I wanted the freedom to move on. We were advised to make a list of everything we owned, all of which I had bought, and divide it equally before meeting with the attorney the next week. We did.

The state determined that I would have custody of the girls; David would pay child support. He asked for freedom to spend time with the girls at his home or mine; I agreed. Because there was agreement, the attorney filed the papers. Our 11-year marriage was over in 1967.

* * *

Much as I liked Gainesville and my teaching position at Santa Fe, I had this itchy desire to get away. This was David's town, and soon he would own our house. I wanted to stay in Florida so the girls could visit their dad and I could collect child support. I don't remember how I landed my next job, but it was a winner: Nova Oceanographic Research Institute in Fort Lauderdale, as a chemist in a lab on a houseboat docked at Pier 66 right off the beach.

Janet would have to move, too. She put in an application with Nova and landed a job in their Education Department. Luck was with us, as we had a good thing going with our "family arrangements." Nova even paid our moving expenses.

My job there was similar to the first job I ever had, measuring minerals, this time in seawater instead of vegetables. The lab equipment was modern and the personnel friendly. And I got to look the part wearing a lab coat.

Janet and I found a roomy house close by with a grassy yard and a big backyard tree with a rope swing. We enrolled Scott in elementary school and the others into a Montessori preschool and kindergarten. Sundays, we'd pile into Janet's Chevy Nova with sand buckets, towels, a cooler of food, sunscreen, and head for the beach, singing along with tunes on the radio. We found a perfect spot with calm water near a jetty where Scott could fish and the younger ones could swim safely. Sometimes the beach regulars would stop and dig in the sand with the kids.

Once a month or so, we'd drive to Gainesville so the kids could visit their dads. One Christmas, the dads both came to Fort Lauderdale. They put together a giant jungle gym kit from Sears.

Janet was so friendly that it wasn't long before we had a lively social life. I hung on for the ride, still shy, born a loner I guess.

Chapter 19: Tough Choice

Nova threw a New Year's Eve party for all the staff: fancy food, champagne, and a real live band. Spirits were high with everyone singing and kissing at midnight. A physics grad student reached for my hand, and with a smile, led me into a side room and took down my panties. "Why not, I thought. I'm loose as a goose and safe." I'd been taking the pill in hopes of finding a guy who could lead me to orgasm. This guy wasn't the one, same old "Wham Bam, Thank You, Ma'am."

Three days later, I sensed that indescribable feeling that I'd felt before. And then morning sickness. I went to a clinic and got a pregnancy test. Positive. Damn. The pill didn't work.

An instant hit, "the pill" became legal in 1962, however, the failure rate was high, due to insufficient understanding of women's hormonal activity.

I told the physicist father that I was pregnant with his child. He played dumb. Soon I was getting weird vibes from all the guys. The chatter was, "That's what girls do to get a husband."

What now? Clearly, there were two options: have another child or have an abortion. I tried to envision life attempting to raise three kids in a culture that didn't approve of women working, of women getting divorced, of divorced women working, of divorced women with children working. Untenable if one of the kids was illegitimate. Not good.

I researched articles about abortion—this was now 1968: abortions caused 80 percent of maternal deaths in America. Passionate articles debated the morality of the pill, presented arguments over legal vs. illegal abortion, woman's rights. Religious dogma weighed in heavily.

But there were no articles about the woman herself, her life afterward, and coping with another child to feed and raise, or how having an abortion affected her, physically or emotionally.

It surprised me to learn that many cultures didn't have a problem with abortion. Some considered it "prevention." In Russia, women favored abortion over contraceptives for birth control because they considered the latter harmful by disrupting a woman's hormonal function. In Poland, the charge for a hospital abortion was 10 dollars. In Sweden, fetal development was prevented with a pill that induced menstruation.

At that time, abortions were legal in some states with a simple, safe, outpatient procedure called a D&C (dilation and curettage, opening and cleaning the uterus), which was performed in a clinic or hospital. However, abortions of any kind were illegal in Florida.

I heard that some women had abortions done illegally by nurses, midwives, or even did it to themselves with knitting needles or coat hangers. I also learned there were upscale, illegal clinics that performed the D&C. I heard about one upstate that used the fees from "well-to-do" women to pay for abortions for poor women—the Robin Hood of Abortionists.

My boss, the Director of Research, called me into his office. "There are rumors that you're pregnant. Are you?"

"Yes, sir. But I'll be having a D&C so I won't miss a day of work." Can't believe I said that, that it came out so quickly.

"I see," he said with no expression.

I asked around. My friends and their friends asked around. I had my heart set on finding Robin Hood. Time was ticking along. Mom came to me in a dream, "Don't be so picky." I took that to mean that I better do something fast. I encouraged my friends and acquaintances to step up their networking. I even called Dr. Zorch; he was offended, but couldn't find anyone to do it.

I was giving up, resigned to having another child when who should call but David. "I heard you need help. I found Robin Hood."

I thought I was dreaming. "You? David? Is this you?" I was dumbfounded.

"You don't call for an appointment. Just put 250 dollars in an envelope with the pregnancy test results and give it to him. There's no address, but I have a map."

"Would you go with me, please? I'm scared."

❧ Harsh Reality ❧

The map took us into the woods east of Ocala, over four hours straight north of Fort Lauderdale. There it was: an old wood house among the trees with a cross on the porch. Inside were half-dozen black women, not talking. Two kids sat on the floor quietly playing with sticks. The air was thick with the odor of armpits and sour clothes. After a while, a black nurse opened the door, signaling one of the women to come in. Three hours later, I got the signal.

The room was a typical examining room, clean and white. The nurse smiled warmly and patted my shoulder. "The doctor will be in shortly."

Another door opened. A husky black man wearing a white doctor coat came in extending his hand to me. We spoke platitudes for a minute. Then he asked why I had come to see him. I figured this was the moment, so I put the envelope on the table between us. He didn't pick it up but looked hard into my eyes.

"Do you know what this involves?"

"I think so."

"We don't use anesthetic." Silence. "Do you think you can handle it?"

"Yes."

He opened the envelope, counted the bills, and scrutinized the lab report.

"Why haven't you done anything sooner?"

"I tried, but I couldn't find anyone."

He scowled at me. "Who recommended that you come here?"

"A professor friend at the University of Florida."

He handed me a piece of paper. "Print the professor's name."

I did. I didn't tell him the professor was in the waiting room.

"Come back in two days. Bring another hundred dollars." He left the room, and the nurse helped me out the door, my knees shaking and mind racing.

$350 in 1968 is equivalent to $2,450 in 2017.

We were four hours from Fort Lauderdale and less than an hour from Gainesville, so we went there to wait the two days and to get more money. It was strange sleeping on the couch at my old house.

When we returned to the clinic, I was taken right in and shown to another room with an exam table, surgical equipment, and a bright fluorescent lamp.

"Disrobe and put this on," said the nurse handing me a paper gown.

"How long does this take," I asked her.

"Don't worry; the doctor is very good."

I lay back on the table, aware now of my pounding heart and pulsating neck.

The nurse brought in a package of instruments, laid them out on a tray table next to me. The doctor came in, looked over the instrument tray, washed his hands, and put on rubber gloves. Making eye contact, he said with authority, "Now, I need your cooperation for this."

"What do you want me to do?"

"One thing," he said, "just one thing. Don't yell."

"OK."

"Did you hear me? Do you understand what I just said?"

"Yes."

He continued, "I will describe to you what I'm doing, and I will tell you what I want of you as I proceed. It will help a lot if you can relax. And if you can concentrate on relaxing, you'll have a lesser tendency to open your mouth. But no matter what you do, you may not make a single sound, or I'll stop right then, and I won't finish."

He sat down on a stool; I put my feet in the stirrups with the sheet draped over my knees. He lined up his instruments. I lay back, grasping the sheet with one hand because it was perspiring. With the other hand, I held an ammonia vial that I had brought just in case.

"Take a big breath and exhale slowly." The doctor inserted the largest of the instruments and told me this was to hold the cervix sufficiently wide so he could work. He turned the screw knob, which seemed to spread me far beyond normal capacity. I looked at the clock, perspiring now, mind getting fuzzy. It was ten after two. Odd. Two years ago, I had been on a table just like this, delivering Anne at ten after two.

The doctor was speaking now. "You must control yourself. This is going to hurt."

It didn't feel like a needle. It felt like a fire-poker, and it was hot. I watched the second-hand move up the clock and felt the needle move around. The pain was beyond intense, getting broader and more intense. A sharp, penetrating pain. The needle went deeper. The second-hand moved. Four and three-quarters minutes now. The doctor had been talking, but I hadn't been hearing.

Suddenly, the needle was pulled out and warm fluid trickled down my buttocks. The second-hand moved toward the 12. I gripped the sheet, realizing now that I had no feeling in my hands, arms. No feeling in my toes or feet. My nose was cold. I watched the clock. Six minutes now. My limbs tingled.

The nurse said, "You can get up now."

The words fell on my ears, but I couldn't move. She took the ammonia bottle from my hand and put it under my nose. "It's all over." I couldn't move. The nurse called in another woman. They rubbed my hands, arms, legs, and feet briskly. Feeling came back slowly; I felt no pain; I was not in this world.

The doctor came in. "Now, what I have done is distress the tissue."

I became alert. "You mean I haven't passed the fetus?"

"Oh no," he said. "You'll do that within several days, in all probability."

I realized what had just happened. It wasn't a simple, clean-cut D&C at all. It was only a plain backwoods illegal abortion.

"You take these tablets," he said. "They're antibiotics. We can't afford for any infection to set in. Do you have someone to drive you home?" I nodded. "Fine. If you have any trouble, I want to know what it is. You call this number."

David was still in the waiting room, reading. He didn't say anything; I crawled into the back seat of the car and pulled a blanket around me, shivering. I felt the car pull out of the parking lot, onto a dirt road and then pick up speed, heading down the highway. My mind fell away into a vacuum.

Pulling up to my house in Fort Lauderdale, David said, "You're home. Are you OK? I'll walk you inside. I have to get back to Gainesville now." Leaving he said, "I'm sorry you had to experience this." He turned and walked away after the kindest words he had ever spoken to me—compassion I never expected.

∞ Afterward ∞

The next morning, I woke with a dull aching pain throughout my abdomen, telling me not to move. The hours passed as I slept and didn't sleep, wishing this tortured fetus was not in me. I thought of the poor women in the waiting room and was grateful that I had helped them pay for this minimal care. I thought of the many desperate women who did this themselves, dying, unable to cope with the hardship of miserable, demanding lives. I wondered where the men were, the fathers, the ones who impregnated them, probably without their consent.

I helped Janet fix dinner. She'd been a real friend taking care of things. I stayed home the next day and the next. Something should be happening besides blood clots now and then. The third day, I went to work. The fourth day, I went to work. Nothing. Five days now . . . getting nervous. Something's wrong. I walked, did sit-ups, leg raises, and put the paper with the doctor's phone number on the table by my bed.

Early morning on day six, my back ached, getting worse as I struggled to be calm at work. I passed a clot the size of an orange, discerned it was only blood by poking it with the handle of the toilet brush. The backache left.

Day seven. The backache returned. I lay in bed stretching and doing easy crunches when I felt warmth, like pee, run down my rump. And up my back. Oh, my God, my water broke. That stupid doctor didn't tell me about this. I called in sick. But nothing more. I grew scared again. Labor usually starts soon after the water breaks. That night, contractions began, quickly gaining momentum. Staying in the bathroom, I alternated kneeling facing the toilet with sitting on the toilet and pushing with all my belly strength. Yes, I was in pain, but not thinking about it. Just pushing.

And then a glob of mucus came out; milky-white jelly settled into the bottom of the toilet bowl. The pain subsided. Transfixed, I kneeled quietly looking at it. Gingerly, I reached in and scooped it up, holding it carefully. Fluid slipped away through my fingers, and there it was. The fetus, my baby.

Fascinated now, I looked at it under the light, seeing the barest outline of a head shape and translucent bones. Hands? Not sure. I rotated the blob, looking, imagining the whole of it. A surge of warmth and affection for this thing began to fill me, to possess me. It was unreal. I felt love for this thing in my hand. I wanted to press it to my face. I decided that I was probably insane, that I had to let it go. Reluctantly, I let it slip back into the toilet. With tears, I flushed it away.

That peculiar feeling stayed with me for years. Sometimes, a vision came: a boy, a boy looking like his dad, sandy curls, square face, and warm smile: the physicist on the boat. This vision seemed so real. A phantom child growing up, always two years younger than Anne. Once, making sandwiches for the kids' lunch boxes, I unconsciously made one for him, too. On the playground at school, I'd see him wave. In time, the vision faded, leaving much the same way as children grow up and leave home.

Is this crazy? Am I alone? No one knows. Women know better than to talk about these things. Life harbors secrets mere humans may never understand. Better to keep such thoughts to myself.

How do I remember all of this? In the months following the abortion, I wrote everything down as though it were a memoir. I wrote and wrote on yellow pads; then typed it. Not just what happened, but my struggles to understand a culture that dogs women, the caretakers of the world. The writing was cathartic. I saved the papers in an old briefcase, not willing to throw them away. Reading these pages now has brought the experience back to life.

To share it now seems right.

* * *

My life was different, solemn after the abortion. It's hard to explain. But the harsh reality of it burst forth when my boss called me into his office again.

No smile, flat face. "We will no longer be needing your services at the end of your contract."

"We lost our contract?"

"No, we didn't lose our contract. You lost your contract."

Family at Last

Chapter 20: Being Normal

Just as well, I thought. Folks were treating me differently, avoiding me. My bench-chemist job was getting tedious, analyzing the minerals in sea water, day after day. Nowhere to go but down.

I wrote to Johnny Sjostrom, my old boss at Arthur D. Little, asking whether he knew of anyone who might be looking for a research chemist, mainly me. I said that things weren't working out at my current job. I enclosed a small photo of the girls.

Johnny wrote back right away with three possibilities. I wrote to them all and got one response. I applied for an opening for a chemist in the Pathology Department at Mount Sinai Hospital in Miami Beach. Based on Johnny's recommendation, I got the job. The pay was excellent.

I signed a lease with Parkview Point Apartments, not too far up Collins Avenue and just two blocks from North Miami Beach. Our apartment was on the ninth floor with a 180-degree view.

On my first day at work at Mount Sinai, I learned that the research grant had been canceled. "Didn't you get our letter?"

I made a big fuss, and they apologized and kept me on as a phlebotomist for a lot less money and starting at 4 a.m. I had a terrible time drawing blood, sticking people with needles. The staff had me practice on an orange, but it wasn't the same. They sent me to the chemistry lab. Same hours, same pay, and I felt quite at home.

Beth quickly learned how to get Anne dressed and downstairs to meet the nursery school bus at 7 a.m. and get herself to school, just a block away.

Often I had to leave the girls alone, as I didn't know the neighbors or anyone else. From ads in the newspaper, I hired several different women part-time to help me, but they were never reliable. I took on a poverty mindset so we could pay the rent and also eat. No discount groceries or Walmart back then.

It wasn't all bad. At least we could walk over to the beach on my days off. Beth made friends from school and Anne was a bouncy, happy child.

One balmy evening, as it was getting dark, I came home from shopping, parked, got the groceries out of the car, one bag in each arm, pushed the door shut with my foot, and began walking toward the entrance of the building when a quick breeze came up. It blew my hair and rattled my bags. As I hugged them in, I felt something slither down inside the front of my sundress.

Horrified, I dropped the groceries and screamed, slipping my sundress up and over my head as fast as I could, jumping up and down, right there in the parking lot. Someone picked up my sundress and shook it. A huge cockroach scampered out and ran away.

"It's just a palmetto bug," a man said calmly, looking into my eyes. "They don't hurt people."

My heart was still pounding when I realized I was in my undies and standing in a pile of squashed and scattered food.

Several people came around and were standing about awkwardly. "What happened?"

"A palmetto bug went down her dress. Scared her." The man handed me my sundress, smiling slightly beneath his big mustachio. To the rest, he said, "Help me pick up these groceries, and we'll take them to her apartment."

I hugged my dress to cover my breasts, and we all went upstairs.

Beth opened the door. "Oh, Hi, Mr. Dani," she said smiling, seeming not to notice that I was undressed or the folks bringing in groceries. When they all left, she announced, "That's Mr. Dani. He's the new doorman. Everyone likes Mr. Dani."

An opening came up in Cardiology on the graveyard shift: 11 p.m. to 7 a.m. I asked Mr. Dani if he would babysit the girls on the nights that I would be working since he went off duty at 11 p.m. He agreed, so I took the Cardiology position and got a raise.

My job was to handle emergencies, like arterial blood analysis (a tool used by physicians to direct patient treatment) and preparing the room for cardiac catheterization. (This is a diagnostic procedure in which a catheter, a long tube, is inserted into an artery or vein in an arm, leg, or groin and threaded through the blood vessel into the heart. At the head of the catheter, a camera relays images back through the catheter to a monitor on the ceiling.) Also, I checked all heart monitors in patient use throughout the hospital several times a night.

Most challenging was that not much happened at night, and we were not allowed to nap, do busy-work (like knit), nor read non-work-related books or magazines. My lab partner, a graduate student, and I came upon a plan that worked for years: one of us would keep watch down the long hall to our lab, sounding an alert should a staff person approach, while the other either studied (him) or napped (me).

Over time, Dani and I became friends. He was soft-spoken, an upbeat kind of guy, seven years my senior. When he was five years old, he and his 3-year old brother had been left at a church in Cabo Rojo, Puerto Rico, by his mother who then disappeared. The nuns found his father in Spanish Harlem running a corner grocery store with his wife. He came for the boys. Dani's job at home was to get his five siblings fed and ready for school in the morning. After school, he learned boxing at the Police Academy gym and played the steel pans in a street band.

Dani joined the Navy at age 17. He was assigned to an aircraft carrier and sent to fight in the Pacific Theater. Wounded in the Philippines, he received the Purple Heart. After WWII, he joined the Army to box on their boxing team, traveling the globe. He was proud that he had crossed the equator 17 times.

After that, Dani became a cook. He owned The Puerto Rican Spaghetti Café on Miami's South Beach with his wife until they divorced, which was when he came to Parkview Park Apartments as the head doorman.

One day, Dani said, "I'd like to make love to you."

"Not if you have a big dick," came out of my mouth by surprise.

"I don't, but it's bent."

"What do you mean, it's bent?"

"Well, halfway down it takes a right turn, sort of." He made me laugh.

"I'll think about it." I was beginning to like Dani's easy ways, positive attitude, and humor.

I thought for a couple of months while re-charting my monthly rhythm cycle. I hadn't had reason to use prevention since the abortion, and I sure wasn't going to trust pills ever again.

The Rhythm Method

There are many variations of the Rhythm Method, but here are the basics, as we knew them:

A woman's body temperature is lower during the first part of the menstrual cycle. Between 14 and 18 days into the cycle, a woman ovulates, releasing her egg. Her temperature rises and peaks at that time. Then it drops for the remainder of the period, but not as low as it was at the beginning. It falls again just before the next period begins, usually on days 26 to 28.

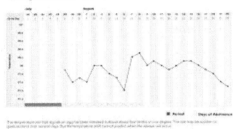

Temperature Chart

The "safe" days for unprotected sex are days 6 to 13 and again 3 to 4 days after ovulation until the end of the cycle when menstruation returns. "Safe" is a general guide, not a promise. It is advisable to chart your personal rhythm for as many months as needed to establish consistency.

We would chart our cycles on graph paper, either store-bought or made with a ruler and pencil: 31 days on the horizontal axis. On the vertical axis, we recorded our temperature in tenths between 97 and 100 degrees. Upon waking in the morning, barely moving, we would reach for the thermometer and put it under the tongue for about five minutes. Then read and record.

The cyclical temperature pattern varies among women but is pretty consistent for a single female. Illness, stress, and restless sleep will affect the accuracy.

∽ Family Life ∽

There was no particular event or time when Dani became family with the girls and me and into my bed. Making love was fresh and new for me; orgasms happened. It was all so easy: no stress, no demands, no problems. Tender time exploring positions together. Discovering the moment. Slowly riding the wave, making it last, then crashing down into ecstasy. Resting in pure joy.

Finally, I understood why the cultural talk about orgasm was elusive, guarded. When honored, a woman's emotions during orgasm defy description; the depth of bonding with one's partner has no parallel. The moment is sacred. When disrespected, it is emotionally and physically painful. When seen as a man's "right," a means to "dump his wad," "have a couple minutes of action," for power, control, an outlet for anger or frustration, orgasm likely cannot/will not happen for a woman. My 10 years of "Wham Bam, Thank You, 'Ma'am" with David was not only callous but was a culturally endorsed form of abuse.

Our new family ate breakfast and dinner together and carried our lunches in lunch boxes.

I made breakfast from eggs: poached, scrambled, fried, sunny-side up, or over easy with bacon, ham, or cheese. Dani made omelets on Sunday. Often, we'd have rice instead of toast or biscuits. Always juice or fruit.

Dinners were Puerto Rican core: pork chops, black beans and rice with fresh vegetables and salad in season, often with avocado, mango, or papaya. Dani would make saffron rice with shrimp or Puerto Rican Spaghetti (a.k.a. Spaghetti Made by a Puerto Rican). On special occasions, we would slow-roast pernil (pork shoulder) seasoned with adobo. On Sundays, we had flan for dessert.

When it was time to renew my lease, Parkview Point said, "NO." I did not have the appropriate moral standards to be a tenant there. Sleeping with the doorman. How crass.

We found a basic three-bedroom house with a Florida room (sunroom) in a well-tended neighborhood in North Miami. The girls bunked together, and the third bedroom became a playroom. On the covered porch on the back of the house, Dani set up his boxing gear: speed bag and heavy punching bag. He was thrilled. An old, convoluted banyan tree in the backyard was so huge that Dani built the girls a tree house, high up. The girls were excited. We got a Lassie dog for Beth, a Chihuahua for Anne.

Beth loved her new Lassie dog, baseball, and school. Anne was happy taking dancing and acting lessons and playing with her Barbies.

Anne was having trouble in first grade, however. She couldn't connect letters with words. Déjà vu: the same problem I had in Miss Roseberry's first-grade class. Anne's teacher told us about a research study going on at a local college. Anne was accepted and was diagnosed as having "Minimal Brain Dysfunction," an impressive name, but with no solution.

We sold our cars: Dani's T-Bird and my Karman Ghia and bought a used, forest green VW bus so we could all fit into one vehicle. In keeping with the fashion of the day, Dani converted the inside of the bus into a camper with storage bins for food and clothing and a table that swung up in front of the back seat. I put up curtains fashioned from orange fish netting and attached dried starfish and sprigs of dry seaweed. We put a "Save the Environment" decal in the back window.

Sometimes, we went camping in the Smoky Mountains. Friday nights, we went to the boxing matches in the Miami Arena. We saw Cassius Clay fight once and Louis Rodriguez fight several times. We frequented live music events. In 1969, we took the girls to see *Hair: The American Tribal Love-Rock Musical*. At the finale, the actors came into the audience, grabbing folks to come up on stage to dance; Beth got caught and joined the "Be-In." What a thrill! Yes, we were "wanna-be hippies," but way too old, with children and real jobs. We watched Woodstock on TV.

Evenings, we watched shows like *Sonny and Cher*, *Flip Wilson*, *Laugh-In*, *I Love Lucy*, *Andy Williams*, *The Waltons*. We'd crowd up together on the couch.

Life was good.

"I would like to have a son." Dani took me by surprise.

"Oh, I don't think so," I responded. "I couldn't possibly take on anything else, and besides, I'm almost 39, too old to have a baby."

"But, I want to have a son."

"You're 46; you're too old, too."

Over the next few months, Dani was despondent. Deep down, I longed for a son, too. My aborted boy child still haunted me. Acutely aware that the chance was 50-50 for a boy, I stopped charting my rhythm, just let nature take its course. I didn't know how we would handle the daily grind but knew that Dani would do whatever it took to make life easy for us. I didn't say anything until I knew I was pregnant. He was ecstatic, dancing up and down, whooping and hollering.

It was time to get married. And tell Mom. Dad had died the year before from a collapsed lung; he'd always had asthma. I had avoided marriage, as I was never sure whether I wanted to be married again, and knew the family would be upset. I called Mom.

"What!" In a panic, she asked, "You're going to marry that dark-skinned, illiterate, Catholic foreigner?"

"Mom, he's not a foreigner. He's Puerto Rican."

"He's illiterate!"

"Mom, calm down. Dani has been in the Navy and the Army. He traveled the world, lived in England and India, has owned businesses, and speaks two languages."

"How could you do this to us? You're humiliating our family."

"Mom, Dani has been helping me raise the girls. He's been a blessing in my life."

"I'm going to be sick. Don't you EVER bring Dani to *my* town. I don't want any of my friends knowing what you've done. They'll think I was a terrible mother."

This was no time to tell her that Dani and I were expecting.

Mom and Dad hadn't liked David either in the beginning. I had thought they would as he met their criteria for an appropriate husband: debonair, polished social skills, respectable parents, intelligent and educated. But Mom called him a "stuffed shirt." Dad suggested he might be a "'fruit." They eventually accepted him.

There at Mount Sinai, I could work my job until delivery and then get two weeks off (unpaid). On a Friday, just after dinner, I felt labor begin. Within an hour, contractions were coming on fast. Dani and I jumped into the VW; I lay down on the floor hanging on to a 40-pound bag of dog food as he spun out of the driveway, heading for the freeway. He put on the flashers, leaned on the horn, and went flying down the highway toward the hospital. A 30-minute drive in 20 minutes. He swerved into the emergency entrance, honking. Two ER nurses slid me onto a gurney and pushed fast. "The head's showing," shouted one of them. I hung on and passed out.

Consciousness returned upon hearing Dani shouting, "It's a boy! It's a boy!"

The nurses were tending to the baby, and the doctor was pulling on the placenta. He smiled at me and said, "You could help. Push." A couple of my co-workers were there, smiling and clapping.

We named the baby Yano, not Charles Edward nor Juan Carlos. Something unique. He was a jolly little (six-pound) fellow, the center of attention.

Despite all our plans and efforts, I grew overly tired, still working the graveyard shift. I slept only while the girls were in school, but was always interrupted: lawnmowers, doorbell, the phone.

Home-based answering machines were not available until the early '80s.

We found a helper for me from the classifieds. Pearl came twice a week to do laundry and straighten up. But still, I couldn't get enough sleep: I hurt all over. My mind was fuzzy and I started missing work.

Dani took on an extra job selling Steed, an oil conditioner to improve gas mileage.

The Whole Earth Catalog was touting communal living in conjunction with the Back-to-the-Land Movement. I researched communes (groups of people living together and sharing possessions and responsibilities). I was intrigued, longed for fresh air, sunshine, gardening, and like-minded folks. Dani had heard that California weather was a lot like the weather in Puerto Rico. Beth wanted a place big enough for a pony or horse. Anne was struggling in second grade, about to fail. We all dreamed of having better lives somewhere else.

Chapter 21: Back to the Land

Like a gift from heaven, Dani was offered a managerial position in Steed's new office in Woodland Hills, in the San Fernando Valley, just north of Los Angeles. He had been making good sales, and they needed a bilingual representative. We quit our jobs and said, "Goodbye." The hospital gave me a tiny lapel pin inscribed with 'Mount Sinai Hospital of Greater Miami' in appreciation for my five years of service. (I still have it.)

With high expectations, we sold most of our stuff, bought a pull-along pop-up trailer, packed up essentials, three kids, two dogs, and a cat, and headed west. It was a memorable two-week trip, camping along the way. We pulled into Los Angeles the summer of 1973.

The closest commune was 50 miles from Los Angeles. We couldn't do both; the position with Steed was the obvious choice. We found a small, old two-bedroom house with a screen porch and a big pool on half an acre of fertile soil and fruit trees in Panorama City, mid-valley. It was near schools and a Veteran's Administration (VA) hospital that would honor my Florida lab tech license. Perfect. Beth could have a horse; a Performing Arts School for Anne wasn't too far away. I could garden. I even telephoned Dr. Zorch, the psychiatric resident in Gainesville, to thank him again and tell him how happy I was.

We had just moved in when the California Attorney General closed Steed down. I don't remember why.

Dani got a job at a nearby 7-11 convenience store, the night shift. Soon he got a better one at a gas station, daytime. I got on as a lab tech at the VA Hospital: 30 hours per week. Dani applied for Carl's Jr. Management Training and performed well. They assigned him to a restaurant near us. We registered the girls in school, tilled and mulched the soil for a spring garden, and settled into our new life together.

It didn't take Dani long to find a Puerto Rican community in Los Angeles. Soon he was a regular for Friday night social events. He also joined a bowling team. I was happy having private time. Our first home project was to build a big shed to house tools, a horse, and chickens. We all pitched in.

Beth soon found a spunky pony, animal-crazy friends, and a girls' softball team. It didn't take Anne long to get busy in show business: acting lessons led to a personal manager, then an agent, then commercials, five of them in her first year. Anne's school placed her in a "handicapped students" classroom, which we hoped would be better for her. Yano, now 18 months old, slept in our room.

Anne was more miserable than ever in the classroom for handicapped students. The principal had no solution to offer her. I made an appointment with the Los Angeles Area School District Office. They had nothing to offer kids with "Minimal Brain Dysfunction." They suggested Laurence, a private school that might work for her. It was perfect; she enrolled and blossomed.

The weather was so warm that we didn't need a greenhouse to sprout seedlings for later planting. Instead, we turned two bags of topsoil into an old flower bed against a white brick wall facing the sun and away from the street. We seeded vegetables and some marijuana we had brought from Florida: Jamaican Bush and Panama Red.

One day, I made a U-turn in front of the theater downtown, going to pick up the girls from the movie. I didn't see the "No U-Turn" sign and was pulled over by the police. They made me and the girls sit on the curb while they searched our bus. Apparently, they didn't trust us: probably our colorful bus or maybe my Stevie Nicks dress. They dumped out all the drawers and used a whisk broom and dustpan, sweeping the floor. I kept a few first aid supplies: band-aids, mercurochrome, aspirin, in a top drawer. When one of the police picked up a small jar of white powder

from there, I said, "That's baking soda. I have it to treat burns or insect bites when we go camping." He glared at me. They talked among themselves for a moment. One put his finger in the powder and touched it to his tongue. I had a hard time not laughing at the look on his face. It was baking soda.

We went straight to the house and pulled up the marijuana plants, stuffed them in garbage bags, and buried them behind the shed. The police never came.

In early Spring we planted a vegetable garden following the *Old Farmers' Almanac* Moon Calendar: above-ground veggies are planted in daylight during the waxing of the moon; below-ground veggies are planted at night during the waning of the moon.

Plus 15 marijuana plants, several varieties.

At Easter, we bought a dozen chicks, good layers: Rhode Island Reds, and California Whites.

By late spring, the marijuana plants were taller than the corn. We had learned that law enforcement helicopters patrolled the valley looking for backyard plants, easy to spot owing to their unique color of green. I disguised ours by attaching bright red crepe paper flowers near the tops. I learned how to make them in college when decorating floats for the Homecoming Parade.

But alas, we lost our marijuana plants anyhow. On the Fourth of July, we had a neighborhood cookout and swim party at our place, and by the next morning, the plants were missing. The thieves weren't so smart, as the plants had not yet budded.

College Homecoming Parade Float

To construct our float, we first molded chicken wire into the basic structural design, like a huge Wildcat (our mascot), on a long truck bed. For weeks, students gathered whenever they had time and made the flowers: a 3-inch by 6-inch piece of crepe paper twisted at the center and secured there with a thin wire. When thousands of such flowers were ready, and usually the day and night before the parade, they were attached to the wire structure on the flatbed until flowers covered everything.

☙ The Worm Farm ☙

In *The Los Angeles Times*, I read that the Department of Sanitation planned to use red worms to reduce a growing garbage problem. They needed red worms to seed the garbage pits. Eager to connect with the Back-to-the-Land Movement, I signed us up to raise worms for the project. We built 60 worm beds of four-by-eight-foot three-quarter-inch plywood secured on the corners with two-by-fours and hinged at the top. We installed automatic sprinklers across the top of the beds to keep the beds moist.

We bought an open trailer to pull behind the VW and procured manure from Alta Dena, an organic dairy. The bedding was half manure and half peat, which we got from a garden shop nearby. When all was in place, we seeded the beds with worms and watered them down. Daily, we layered manure, lime, and walnut meal on top and watered it in. The worms proliferated, and within a few months, they were ready to harvest.

Early in the morning when the worms came up to the surface to feed, we would scoop out the top layer, lay it on a two-foot-square screen, and gently shake it until the bedding fell through. We put the worms into carrying bins of moist peat and took them to collection sites for sale.

As the worms grew, they left their castings (worm poo) behind. The level of castings deepened in the beds in time. To clean out the beds, we moved the worms to a fresh bed and shoveled the castings into a wheelbarrow. We dried them in the sun, ground them up with a big, motor-driven grinder, and bagged them for sale as fertilizer at gardening stores.

Raising worms was physically exhausting and earned precious little. Within a year, the project was cancelled to the disappointment of many dedicated worm-growing environmentalists. When we stopped feeding the worms, they moved on to gardens all over the neighborhood.

We didn't tear down the beds hoping the City would change their minds, which they didn't. It was years before we gave up and had a friend with a Bobcat make berms with the castings for Yano (about age 10) and his friends to practice their dirt-bicycling tricks.

Chapter 22: Turmoil

↝ Losing Mom ↝

Santa Barbara wasn't that far up the 101 from Panorama City. I yearned to see my mom, but stubbornly wouldn't visit her without the family, the whole family. She agreed to meet us at "The Big Yellow House," a restaurant in Summerland, far enough away from Santa Barbara that she was sure none of her friends would see us. Mom was uncomfortably cordial, Dani was shyly charming, and the kids were a great distraction, especially the busy two-year old.

The following Christmas, 1974, Mom came to visit us for several days. We had a lovely time; a healing time.

In January, Mom had a paralyzing cerebral stroke. Back at home, she had awakened from a mid-afternoon nap and, getting up, got her feet tangled in the covers. She fell forward and hit her head on the corner of her dresser.

Mom's sister found her unconscious and called an ambulance. The stroke caused sufficient paralysis that they recommended she go to a care facility. Mom could not communicate nor take care of basic needs. The kids and I went to see her. She sat in a wheelchair by a sunny window, dressed in a flowered wrap-around. Her hair was combed up with a pink bow. She smiled at us without recognition. She did not notice when we touched her. She smiled sweetly watching her three-year old grandson skip around energetically. It was heartbreaking.

Mom died on the 4th of July. She was 69. I see me now sitting on the stoop of our front porch with my head in my hands. Unable to process this. I felt a deep pain in my chest. Dani sat down beside me, saying nothing, just holding me. When Dad had died five years earlier, I was sad and went to the funeral and cried. But losing Mom was different, as though part of me had been ripped away.

Mom had requested cremation, no funeral, no family or friends gathering.

ஒ Losing Dani ஒ

A few months later, I was walking by Dani's bathroom. (He was a private-kind-of guy. I didn't mind sharing the other bathroom with the kids.) I stopped short at hearing a whimpering kind of sound from inside. I knocked. "Dani, is everything all right?"

"Of course," was his convincing reply.

A few days later, I heard it again. I put my ear to the door. Something wasn't right. I opened the door. Dani was sitting on the pot, red-faced. "Something's wrong. I heard you."

"Get out."

"No. You tell me what's going on."

"I'm having trouble pooping, that's all. Now get out."

"Lean forward. Let me see it." I pushed his shoulder forward and down and was surprised that he let me. "Dani, there's blood in the toilet."

"I know, but it's nothing. It'll go away."

"Maybe not. This isn't good, Dani. You need to see a doctor."

"No. I hate doctors."

Twice I made appointments for him at the clinic down the street. Twice he didn't show up. I had to trick him. One day, I drove to his work just as he was to get off. "Dani," I yelled out the window, looking hysterical. "Dani, something terrible has happened. Can't talk about it. No time. Quick, get in." He did.

"What is it; is everyone OK?"

"Can't talk now; gotta concentrate on driving." I pulled into the clinic's parking lot, got out quickly, and ran for the door. He wasn't far behind.

"Who? Who's hurt?"

"Dani is here for his appointment," I said to the receptionist.

"You bitch," he said, the only time he ever called me a bad name.

"You can come right on in," said the stern receptionist. "We've been expecting you."

We both went in. I wasn't going to leave him. He'd probably lie to the doctor or try to escape a side door or something. But Dani was quiet, cooperative. When the exam was over, the doctor said candidly, "We need to take a deeper look. I'm admitting you to the Encino Hospital. I want you to be there at six o'clock in the morning. Don't eat or drink anything else today or in the morning. You can wet your mouth, but don't swallow."

It was a long night. We didn't talk at all. We were up at 4:30 a.m. and early to the hospital. I hugged him as he went in, waited for hours in the reception room.

The doctor came out. "Your husband is in recovery. He had a constriction in his colon. We removed that part of the colon and reconnected it with dissolving sutures. We'll keep him here for a few days. When he is home, give him only soft foods for several weeks. I've taken tissue for a biopsy to look for the possibility of cancer. Depending on the results, we may want to administer radiation therapy."

Cancer?

When the results of the biopsy were in, the doctor talked to us together. The biopsy showed cancerous tissue. Dani was to come in every six weeks for radiation therapy starting the next week. We were to return for a re-exam in six months.

We didn't tell the kids. We moved through the next six months with a positive attitude, though the treatments were incredibly painful for him. Watching him suffer, I had to hold back my tears. When we went back in for his six-month check-up, the doctor did more testing then told us that, apparently, the radiation therapy had not been effective. Dani was to go back to the hospital to have more of his colon removed.

This time, Dani went to the VA hospital where I worked. The time before, we had been so harried that we hadn't remembered that he was a vet. This surgery was scheduled for early July 1976.

When the doctor came into the room to talk with us the day after surgery, I cranked up the head of Dani's bed and climbed in beside him. We held hands.

"I'm sorry to have to tell you this, but when we opened you up," he looked at Dani, "we found that the cancer had metastasized so extensively, well, there was nothing we could do." Dani and I felt each other's devastation, tightened our grip. "Your time is short," he continued. "We know you're in intense pain. We've given you a colostomy so you can evacuate yourself easily."

I felt hollow inside. Dani wasn't moving.

"We'll keep you here so we can manage your recovery and provide palliative medication."

I lay my head on Dani's shoulder; he rested his head on mine.

The doctor left saying, "If you need anything, there's a call button attached to your bed."

There are no words to express the anguish we shared. Our auras meshed. We were one in pain.

I had to tell the kids. I can't remember what that was like. I'm sure it was incredibly difficult. I do remember that Yano, just 5, did not understand. I also remember that the kids wanted to visit Dad in the hospital. We went, but Anne and Yano couldn't see him.

"No one under 12 is allowed to go in," said a big nurse guarding the door.

"But, these are Dani's children."

"Sorry, but those are the rules. No exceptions."

The visitor's room was on the second floor with a window facing a narrow street behind the hospital. A grassy hillock beneath the window was just high enough that I could touch the windowsill. So I would pick Yano up after kindergarten, park my car against the curb in front of the hillock, and boost Yano onto my shoulders. Dani waited inside. They would make faces and kiss each other through the glass. That helped, but not much.

"I want to go home," said Dani. "I don't care about the pain; I just want to go home. The Pink Ladies don't work that well anyhow." (Pink Ladies are a drug cocktail thought to contain lidocaine and morphine.)

We made a plan. I would buy a recliner and side table for him and put them in the "den," a garage conversion we had been working on that opened up to both the living room and kitchen.

I told the head nurse I was taking Dani home.

"Oh, no, you can't do that. We have Mr. Anaya in our care. Only the doctor can authorize us to release him."

"I understand," I said. "Where can I find the proper doctor?"

"He's out of town. I don't know when he'll be back."

Dani and I made a new plan. I would park the van in front of the hillock, side door open. I'd come into the visitor's room. Dani and I would take a leisurely walk around the room and slip out the door. Instead of turning right to the front door, we'd go left into a housekeeping service area, down the ramp, and out the back door to the waiting van.

As we exited the back door, we could hear commotion upstairs, but our plan worked.

Family life began anew. The kids were great; they sat with him, Yano scrunched in beside him in his chair. Dani loved his chair. It was soft velour, cinnamon brown. He could sit up or lie way back. The table beside the chair was the right height that he could eat his meals from there. Except for using the bathroom, Dani lived in his chair.

The staff at the hospital forgave me and gave me supplies and Pink Ladies. Tough old military man that he was, Dani took care of his personal self, colostomy included. But he was losing weight and hair. His pain was intense; I'd hear him cry in the night, calling for his mother.

I telephoned Dani's family in New York asking if Dani's mother would come to California to be with him. She agreed. I sent a ticket. When I went to LAX to get her, I waved a picture of Dani at the passengers coming off the plane. A short, chunky lady with white hair, rushed up and hugged me. "Carolina?"

"Yes."

I smiled and hugged her back. "Maumee?"

"Si."

It was now September. I gave our bedroom to Maumee. I bunked with Yano on his narrow bed; we managed, even with his weenie dog in bed with us. Maumee took over the kitchen and shooed me out. She spent long hours with Dani, massaging him and chatting in Puerto Rican Spanish. Maumee was a blessing.

By November, Dani's pain was constant. I telephoned Dr. Zorch. He said, "I'm going to San Francisco to attend a meeting but will swing by your place first and work with Dani. Is Thanksgiving weekend OK?"

Dr. Zorch taught Dani self-hypnosis, spending the whole weekend perfecting the technique so Dani could hypnotize himself at will. Dani's pain subsided; his mood improved. He was never pain-free, but it was bearable. I never saw Dr. Zorch again.

At work, our Laboratory Supervisor retired. A new one came on board on December 1st. He wanted to see me. He greeted me with a handshake; my file was on his desk. "I see you're working here under a Florida license. I called you in to let you know that the Veterans' Administration now requires that all technical staff be federally licensed."

My mind said, "What? Are you kidding me? What are you talking about?"

As if he had heard my mind, he said, "In other words, on January 1st, you'll no longer be qualified to do the job you're now doing. I suggest you get your federal license." He stood, smiled, and handed me my termination notice.

My mind railed. "This is unbelievable. What else can happen?" But then I backed off. "Perhaps I shouldn't ask."

With new eyes, I surveyed my family, three children, a dying husband and his mother, all depending on me for support, emotional and monetary. Now no job, emergency savings practically gone. I decided to keep it to myself. For now. Change was clearly forthcoming.

Christmas was meager: we gave each other handmade/homemade gifts. Maumee made cookies. Beth gave "clouds" hand-stitched from sheeting, stuffed with cotton, fitted with a string to hang them above our beds. Anne tied ribbons around bouquets of backyard weeds. Yano gave up his "best" marbles. I gave foot massages. Dani smiled: a great gift.

January came with rain. Dani took a downturn. He asked me to call the VA's priest to give him his last rites.

> ## Last Rites
> *The last rites are meant to prepare the dying person's soul for death by providing absolution for sins by penance, sacramental grace and prayers for the relief of suffering through anointing, and the final administration of the Eucharist, known as "Viaticum."*

The priest came the morning of January 17th. He delivered the last rites. It was beautiful.

Dani then spoke to Yano. "I have to go now, son. You are now the man-of-the-house. Take good care of your mother and your sisters. I will be with you in spirit forever." They looked deeply into each other's eyes.

"OK, Dad."

Dani surveyed the rest of us, the teary-eyed women in his life, smiled and said, "Thank you." Then he slept.

We woke him for dinner. Maumee had prepared yellow corn-meal mush for him, a childhood comfort food. Halfway through dinner, Dani grasped the right side of his neck and gurgled, eyes wide. We rushed to him. Maumee cradled his head from behind, speaking softly into his ear. Beth on one side, Anne on the other, they massaged his arms and legs. I took Yano to the bedroom, told him it was his bedtime, to stay there.

Oh God, why did I do that? Did I think he couldn't take it? Was I afraid there would be double drama? I've never forgiven myself.

Dani became calmer. He and I smiled at one another. Time moved slowly. "His feet are getting cold, Mom," said Beth. I wiped his brow, thanked him for showing me respect and true love. Maumee stroked his face, weeping quietly.

"His legs are starting to get cold, Mom," said Beth.

"His hands are getting cold, Mom," said Anne.

"So are his arms," said Beth

Then, Dani's eyes became unusually bright for 10 or more seconds, then slowly began to fade. After he sighed deeply, the light left his eyes; they looked like cardboard. His chest relaxed. He twitched but did not move. I called the VA. They came and took him to the hospital. He was pronounced dead at 3:30 a.m. on January 18, 1977. Only 51.

Dani wanted cremation; a year and a half earlier he had been a handsome, proud, robust man and that's how he wanted his family and friends to remember him. Not this way: colorless, hairless, and emaciated with sunken eyes and dry scaling skin that cream wouldn't soften. The VA offered cremation and a simple service that had to be handled right away. I called family and friends.

There was a supportive turn-out at the VA chapel: Dani's friends from work, Anne's manager, a few of our new neighbors, Maumee, of course. Dani's daughter and son from his WWII days 35 years earlier, flew in from New York. After the service, most of us went to The Los Angeles National Cemetery in Westwood where Dani's ashes were interred with a special ceremony then back home where friends had brought light snacks.

Dani's daughter and son were upset that there had been no viewing, that the chapel was so small, that I hadn't gotten a hotel for them. I felt bad for them until I realized that when they left, they had taken all of Dani's personal things, except for his dirty clothes in the laundry basket. Good thing I was wearing my wedding ring.

Maumee went with them. I hugged her and thanked her and gave her Dani's Purple Heart, WWII certificates, and recent pictures of him. I had grown to love and respect her.

Darkness Into Light

Chapter 23: Slipping Away

Over the next few weeks, I tidied up the house and rearranged a few things, but I was not into it. On purpose, I didn't wonder how I was going to pay the bills or feed us, or the animals. Instead, I bought flats of pansies and johnnie-jump-ups, planted them in beds around the front door. Greg, a kind-hearted high school boy who had worked the worm farm with us, offered to take over Dani's chores, no charge.

Yano sat in Dani's chair. For weeks. Doing nothing.

I met with the principal of the elementary school. He told me he would talk to Yano's kindergarten teacher about him and he shared that her husband had recently passed. She called to offer her support. Yano finally went back to school. His teacher was wonderful with him.

A couple months later, a woman knocked on our door. "I'm from Social Security," she said.

I thought, "What now? Is it tax time or something?"

"Due to the recent death of your husband, you and your children are eligible for survivor's benefits. I am here to answer your questions and assist you in making an application if you haven't done so already."

I had no idea such a thing existed. I invited the woman right in. She encouraged me to petition the court to receive a percentage of Anne's payments from show business, as now it would be entirely on me to enable her career to continue. She encouraged me to file for child support from David, as he had never paid after the first two payments. I had filed in two different states years earlier but to no avail, as there were few laws to support it, but I'd try again anyhow.

Beth was not happy either. She was hit by a car while riding her bike to school. She got in trouble for taking her shoes off in class; they didn't care that she'd had foot problems since birth. She didn't like living in the city and wanted to go to Gainesville, live with her Dad, and finish high school there. She had been visiting David during summers for many years so had friends there. Beth had been my right hand through all our years. I'd miss her terribly. But David was willing; she was 16. I let her go.

Reality struck. Hard. Beth leaving, Dani gone, Mom gone, Dad gone, Aunt Sarah gone, Gramma gone, other Gramma gone. I was alone with two children and no one to reach out to. My brothers and I rarely communicated. Just Christmas cards. I knew I couldn't maintain our place there by myself, so put it all up for sale and scouted the area for a smaller home for just the three of us.

I don't remember the next few years very well. Snippets are all. Janet, my housemate from Florida, came to help out. She took Anne to job interviews and acted as her guardian on the set when she had an acting job.

Pearl, who had helped us with housekeeping right after Yano's birth, came, too. Her daughter had called me from Florida, said Pearl was becoming frail and wanted to see California before she died. It would be good to have Pearl back in my life. I got a small travel trailer for her to live in, as there wasn't room or privacy in the house. I put the trailer out back under a big tree.

Pearl was a staunch caretaker, puttering around, doing dishes and laundry, just like the old days back in Miami. She insisted that I have a lemonade with her after finishing the day's chores. She knew I needed to take time for myself and relax. Slowly, I re-engaged with life.

Show-biz for Anne slowed; Janet left. Pearl went back to Florida. As she was leaving, I asked her for her lemonade recipe, as it sure did the trick. "Three-quarters of a cup of strong lemonade with two jiggers of Puerto Rican Rum," she said.

"Really?" I thought. If David or Dani or I had ever been drinkers, I might have recognized the rum. But we didn't like or drink alcohol. When I was 7 or 8, Mom offered me a sip of her drink at a party at our house. I took a big gulp. I choked and coughed with watering eyes, thought I would die. "That's whiskey," Mom had said. "You can drink it when you're grown up." I knew then I would never drink whiskey or anything like it. Not scotch, not beer, not rum, nor wine.

Surprisingly, I missed Pearl's lemonade. So I began making it for myself. After a few months, I'd have one before bed, too. Soon I would have lemonade in the morning; I wasn't hungry for breakfast. Too much lemonade, I thought. Something with grain would be healthier, like beer. But beer lacked pizzazz. I switched to Mickey's Big Mouth malt liquor. Still missing something. So I put rum in the Mickey's. Perfect. Felt good.

So good in fact, that when a friend, a young guy, flirted with me and asked me to teach him about sex, I perked right up. It seemed natural; older women have been schooling young men about that forever.

In many cultures, historically and current, mature women teaching young men what to do and how to please a woman is the proper way for them to learn as it decreases rape and spares young girls. In raising my son, I advised him to find a mature woman to teach him, which he did. In raising my grandson, I was too late. By age 13, girls had already shown him. Condoms were more about avoiding sexually transmitted diseases than preventing pregnancy.

I enjoyed these "lessons," as he was a kind, gentle soul, so eager to please. It had been a long time since I'd had any affection. I didn't want to let go.

Nothing like alcohol to lower one's inhibitions and make everything seem OK.

But it didn't turn out so well. Anne decided my behavior was sick. Beth thought it was strange. Yes, he was a lot younger than I was. The girls knew of a retired counselor about my age and asked her to talk with me. After an increasingly heated discussion, she stood and barked in my face, "If you want sex so much, why don't you get yourself a husband?"

That wasn't the point, but it was a pivotal moment. It flashed on me that I didn't want another husband, ever. I had had a good one and had had a bad one; that was enough. I surely didn't want some old counselor woman telling me how I should live my life. Nor my children. No one. Leave me alone. I'll figure it out for myself. If I want advice, I'll ask for it.

The property finally sold and I bought a 110-year-old, hand-built, rock and redwood farmhouse with a barn on five-eighths of an acre within walking distance of Yano's school. There were 12 citrus trees in the front yard, an apricot tree and a plum tree out back. Concord grapes grew along the fence by the barn. Bamboo and tropical bananas circled a sagging gazebo and lined the back and side fences giving us privacy. There was a charming rock-edged pool big enough to swim in with a sizable three-room cabana alongside with a kitchen and bathroom. There was plenty of room for a new garden and our chickens.

The living room had an entryway and a rock fireplace, a kitchen and breakfast nook fashioned from pine slabs, and two bedrooms and two baths. A converted attic room with windows on three sides was perfect for Yano.

I parked Pearl's travel trailer in the back of the property and the pop-up tent behind the barn and proceeded to find occupants. Jim, a quiet, long-distance truck driver, rented the trailer. Rick, a pool maintenance guy, rented the pop-up trailer. Irene, a husky, no-nonsense FedEx driver, rented the cabana. That brought in a tidy bit to supplement our Social Security checks.

Anne and Yano began talking secretly and wouldn't tell me why. Thinking about it, I realized I had started hiding from them when they came home from school because I was tipsy. Like in the barn or the laundry closet, under the pile of dirty clothes. "Where's Mom?" Anne would ask Yano, and then they would titter.

Yano, now 9 years old, came into the kitchen where I was cooking dinner for them and wrapped his arms around my waist. Looking up at me with big brown eyes, he said, "You don't have to worry when you die, Mom. Billy's mom said I could come live with them."

I scoffed. "I'm not going to die, Yano."

He dropped his arms. Looking down, he left the room.

Being in denial, I wondered why he said that.

That very evening, when the kids had gone to bed, I turned on the TV. A commercial was showing a house imploding. "Is your life falling apart?" "Are you confused?" "Do you feel out of control?" It was an advertisement for a rehab clinic. There it was. I got it. I finally got it. Stabbed me right in the heart.

Amazing how deceptive alcohol addiction can be.

The next day, I looked in the phone book for Alcoholics Anonymous. Conveniently, there was an AA meeting in the breakout room of the grocery store just two blocks away. I went that evening. A dozen people were there, sitting around a table, smiling. A man at the head of the table said, "My name is Charlie, and I'm an alcoholic."

The group responded, "Hi, Charlie."

Then, "My name is Jane, and I'm an alcoholic."

Everyone said, "Hi, Jane."

And so it went around the table until it came to me. "Hi, I'm Caroline, and I just came to see what this was all about."

They all said, "Hi, Caroline," in a most friendly way.

The meeting got underway with readings and sharing stories. In the end, we said The Lord's Prayer and then, holding hands in a circle, said,

"Keep coming back. That's what works." We shared a cake, and they chatted, but I had to leave. It was all too new and hard to process.

As I walked to my car, a short, little lady tapped me on the shoulder. "Here," she said, handing me a scrap of paper. "This is my phone number. The next time you feel like you need a drink, don't. Call me."

"That might be at four in the morning," I replied sarcastically.

"I'll be expecting your call." She smiled and walked away.

It was closer to 5 a.m., but I called the number. Talking with the lady was easy. "It can slip up on a person," she said. "And the last person to recognize it is you. Alcohol is cunning, powerful, and cruel."

"I don't want to be like this, but I have no idea what to do," I said. "I have children. I can't just up and go to some fancy place like on TV."

"You might consider a three-day detox," she continued. "They have one right down the street at the Presbyterian Hospital."

I made an appointment at the hospital and talked with a non-judgmental nurse. She took notes on such things as what I drank, how much, when, whether I smoked, used other medications, legal or not, and personal hygiene habits. She looked them over, consulted with another nurse, and then told me that a three-day detox wouldn't do the job, that I needed their 30-day program.

Damn. I didn't realize I was that far gone but I had noticed the intake nurse flinch ever so slightly when I told her I couldn't eat without being sick.

The hospital admitted me on December 9, 1981. Anne, nearly 16 now, surprised me when she took over at home.

The first three days were physical hell in a single room with a cot, chair, and toilet. A male nurse stood guard at the door so I couldn't leave. I shivered, sweated, and ached. I had the worst headache of my life. They gave me injections—vitamins, they said. I doubted that.

After three days, they let me out of my detox room. Still spacey, I cleaned up and started taking classes about health, exercise, and re-entry into the workplace. I attended meetings on alcoholism. In the cultural mindset of the day, a lack of willpower or weakness of character caused alcoholism. In scientific and medical circles, heredity was considered a possible cause. I started thinking about my family tree and found ancestors who "couldn't hold their liquor." In self-esteem class, I learned that not everyone who drinks is an alcoholic. But the true alcoholic won't necessarily recognize that fact until it's too late. Like with me. No sense in beating myself up about it.

A staff doctor stressed that alcoholism is a progressive disease that cannot be "cured," but must be "maintained." To start drinking again will instantly send you back to the physical and mental state you were at the moment you last stopped drinking. "No, you can never just have one little, itty-bitty drink again," Ever. Period. Or you'll go back to Hell.

On December 24th, they gave me a one-day Christmas pass. Beth had come home for the holidays. The kids had put up a tree and wrapped presents. Christmas morning, I woke to the sound of a bird singing right next to my head, in a gold-colored cage with a red ribbon on top. It was "Toupee," a yellow canary with a black top-knot, their gift to me. A turkey was in the oven. This day was one of the best days of my life.

"This will not be easy," the doctor said as I was nearing the end of the 30-day program. "The toxic effects of alcohol use will take many years to dissipate, and they may never be gone completely. We offer you a voluntary six-month follow-up program to help you adjust to your new sober life."

I signed up. For six months after 'graduation,' I had to attend weekly group therapy sessions and AA meetings three times a week in the auditorium at the hospital. At least 200 people were at the meetings, talking loud, smoking, and eating cookies, cake, and candy bars. There was always a speaker who would tell his or her tale of woe in great detail, for about 20 minutes. It gave me headaches.

Home life and family dynamics were askew. No surprise. Yano, now 10, was running loose, ditching school, and surfing at Santa Monica Beach. I had to rein him in. Anne had liked being in charge. I wanted control back.

It took a while for us to fall into a new pattern.

Eventually, Yano got serious about school. Anne had completed the program at Laurence and been "mainstreamed" into public high school. She studied hard and graduated with honors that year.

Chapter 24: Long Journey Back

At home one day, I walked past a full-length mirror, still naked after a shower. I stopped short. My reflection startled me. I saw a skinny, grey-faced, thin-haired, wrinkly woman who needed a full body make-over. I signed up at the Mid-Valley Gym.

The first day, I snuck in the back door, headed right for the Jacuzzi, and slunk into the water so no one would see me. When it seemed safe, I put on a big terry robe and wandered around. I looked no worse than some of the other patrons.

I saw a scale and stepped on it: 93 pounds. I'd lost 25 pounds while drinking instead of eating. It had taken only two and a half years from the start of rum-laced lemonades to near death.

Clean & Sober

6 Months – Skinny but Smiling   1 Year - Looking Good

Time to get busy. I decided to go to the gym five days a week when the kids were in school. The ladies weight room staff offered complimentary coaching. They were happy to take me on, a nice change for them, helping someone gain weight.

In addition to going to the gym every day, I started doing repairs in this new old house. I soon found out it was too late for the electric. Friends and I were sanding down the kitchen cabinets when we smelled smoke. Flames burst out of the utility closet. We threw water on them and called the fire department; so did neighbors. Five fire trucks were there within 11 minutes. Firemen shot water everywhere.

Most of the house survived, though smoke and water damage made it unlivable. While the clean-up crew was there, we gathered a few friends and went to the 1982 US Music Festival in San Bernardino. Tenting there cost less than renting a motel, and it was a whole lot more fun: Fleetwood Mac, Talking Heads, The Police, Santana, The Cars, Pat Benatar, Jackson Brown, Grateful Dead, among others.

My Experience with Marijuana

Marijuana comes from the buds and leaves of the hemp plant. It has a long and fascinating history. This history is important to know because current popular "information" is fraught with misinformation having more to do with money and politics than with therapeutic or recreational use.

I became aware of marijuana and other medicinal plants in the early '60s when David and I were living in Cambridge, Massachusetts.

At that time, Harvard was a focal point for studies regarding the ethnobotany and psychoactivity of medicinal plants: mescaline, psilocybin, and peyote, as well as marijuana and LSD. Scientists involved included David McClelland, Richard Alpert, Timothy Leary, and Andrew Weil. Behind closed doors, curious students happily volunteered to participate in these studies.

I don't know whether David was one of those curious volunteers, but he tried to talk with me about his discoveries of ways to "expand his mind." I wasn't the least bit interested. Now, if he could come up with something to expand time, I'd be interested; I never had enough time to get everything done. Years later, I tried marijuana, more calming than exciting.

Dani, on the other hand, grew up with "weed." It was common in Spanish Harlem in the '30s, especially popular with the "jazz culture." Dani had no "hippie" connection with his use of weed; he only enjoyed it while relaxing at home and when playing his bongo along with Santana and Sergio Mendes 8-tracks (a magnetic tape sound recording technology that was popular in the United States from the mid-1960s to the late 1970s).

Sometimes I smoked with him for relaxation in the same way some people have a glass of wine. During Dani's illness with cancer, we used marijuana more frequently, medicinally, Dani to alleviate pain, me to mollify stress. After he died, I smoked even more, but as my desire for rum-spiked lemonade escalated to two or three glasses a day, my desire for weed dissipated.

When I quit drinking alcohol and got into my daily fitness routine at the gym, the desire for marijuana disappeared. I felt better from just exercising at the gym than I ever did when drinking or smoking weed.

My instinct was to safeguard my sobriety with personal rules in addition to "No drinking alcohol ever again." They were: 1) No one who has been drinking alcohol is allowed on my property or in my space. 2) Don't go to parties or other social events where people are drinking.

3) Always ask if any food or drink someone offers me contains alcohol. 4) No junk food or beverage. 5) No cigarettes. 6) No drugs of any kind unless it's a matter of life or death. 7) No sex.

In December 2017, I took my 36-year chip at AA, celebrating my 36 years of clean and sober living.

⌘

BOUNCING AROUND
I got itchy for a job

⌘ Security Systems ⌘

Because I had once been a Neighborhood Watch Lady, I got a job selling security systems for Knight Protective Industries in 1984. My job was to sell and install the new "One Touch" security system. By tapping a button on the tabletop base unit, the user could open direct voice communication with the company's emergency services. To make a good sale and decent commission, I'd have to scare the bejeebers out of folks: tell them of break-ins in their neighborhood, suggest they install motion sensors outdoors and more lighting, that they cut back the bushes against their house where burglars hide, that their dog might be a watchdog but home invaders might shoot them.

I just couldn't bring myself to do that.

⌘ Magic Mountain Security ⌘

I quit and took a job at Six Flags Magic Mountain Theme Park just north of Los Angeles as a plain-clothes undercover security officer watching the employees. Each day, I was teamed up with another security officer to walk the grounds, observing employees they suspected of theft, dealing drugs, or being under the influence of something. My partner and I would sit on a bench and chat like tired friends and watch for a while, then move on.

We caught a guy once at the cotton-candy kiosk. He made cotton candy by twirling a cardboard stick around the edges of the sugar spinner. Then he put it into a plastic bag and gave it to the customer. The number of sticks he had left at the end of his shift determined his pay. When a single customer came, he slipped the cotton-candy ball off the stick as he put it directly into the plastic bag, and then used that stick to make another cotton-candy ball. He put that customer's pay into his pocket. After work, security got him, pocket heavy with cash.

Walking the 262 acres of rolling hills eight hours a day, five days a week was exhausting, even with sitting.

ᔪ Car Phones ᔪ

So I got a job selling and installing car phones and the Etak Navigator, a predecessor of GPS. The Etak followed the car's location using a complicated arrangement of sensors on the tires. The computed position showed on a screen by the driver's dash. Installing it in and under cars was a dirty job. But, the boss sent me to sales and networking meetings. Fun.

ᔪ Lifespring ᔪ

At an early morning networking breakfast, I met a guy who was all excited about a "personal effectiveness training program" he was taking called Lifespring. Sounded interesting. He took me to an introductory presentation. I thought might be right for me and could give me perspective, so I signed up for their three-day Basic Training. I found such value in the concepts of the Basic that I later took their week-long Advanced Training and then their three-month Leadership Program. After that, I assisted in staffing the training. Lifespring showed me new ways to know myself, the world, and new possibilities for my life, not with lectures or lessons, but through experiential training—doing "exercises" and sharing our reactions.

One exercise called "Secrets" was profound for me. About 60 students sat in chairs placed in a circle far enough apart that people could not touch one another. The lights were dimmed for a minute while people found a chair. Then the lights were turned off, so it was very dark. The instructor asked us to take a few moments to think of our most carefully guarded secret. Something we may have never told anybody. Then it began. The instructor would signal a person to share their story by tapping them on the back of their shoulder.

One after another, each told their secret. Almost every female voice told about having been raped, usually by her father. Or repeatedly raped. Several male voices said they had been violated. One male voice said he had raped his little sister. Nearly every secret was about rape, except for me. I felt blessed that I had been raped only once. Instead, I said, "I had an illegal abortion and had to deliver the fetus myself then flush it down the toilet." My secret seemed anticlimactically weak compared to the emotional rape stories.

When all stories had been told, boxes of tissues were passed around. When the sobbing had ceased, the lights went on low. Some people said they had no idea so many women had been raped. Most women thought they were the only one, that rape never happened to anyone else. Some felt relief. Some, release from guilt.

For the rest of the training, I noticed a silent bond growing among the women—in their glances, shy smiles, touches. A knowingness.

For the first time, I saw that my New Year's Eve party pregnancy was born of my desire to experience the promised pleasure of orgasm, of my trust in pharmaceutical claims, and maybe just of trust in general.

I saw that my fear of society's scorn against me, and probably my daughters, influenced my choice of abortion rather than birthing a bastard. Tough stuff.

"Hot Seat" was another compelling exercise. Groups were five persons, one in the hot seat. The other four had one minute to comment on the way the target presented him/herself. That day, I had worn a black, short-sleeved sweat suit (it was usually cold in the room). They put me in the hot seat.

The start bell rang; they all spoke at once: "What's with the black? You trying to look sexy or something. Give it up. You aren't. Your clothes don't fit. Trying to hide your flat chest? Why no makeup, you tryin' to melt into the wall? Scared of people? Think someone won't notice you? Don't worry; they don't anyhow. What's with the Little Orphan Annie look? Dumb eyes. Try mascara. You're stiff as a board. No class. Plain Jane. You need dental work."

Since then, only my yoga pants are black. I got stylish glasses and had my deformed teeth straightened and capped. I became a better clothes shopper. But I won't wear makeup; it makes my skin itch. I'd never get a boob job. I am not interested in entertaining creeps who carry their brains between their legs. Gives me the willies.

In Lifespring, we learned several ways to change our attitude: being a "mirror" to a partner; "standing in someone else's shoes;" and my favorite, thinking and saying "I get to" do something instead of "I have to."

The idea that I could change my life by changing my attitude simmered in my thoughts.

Maybe I wasn't really a "loner." True, I had spent time alone in Flagstaff, as Connie was the only school friend close enough that we could walk to each other's houses. After fourth grade, my family moved to Albuquerque where the school was "further along." I felt "retarded." Kids in junior high called me "encyclopedia mouth," avoiding me. I helped Mom at home and hung out brushing horses at the nearby horse stables.

Ninth grade in San Jose, California, had been pretty good, but we moved to Shreveport, Louisiana, that next summer. I had felt "dirty" about that false pregnancy thing. I surely didn't fit socially with the Southern Belles. I had one girlfriend who didn't fit in either and a boyfriend. But I liked school and did well in science classes even though most girls took English and Reading and Arts.

But, still, maybe I wasn't a "loner." Perhaps I just made that up, only saw it that way. How perfect that a Lifespring friend shared a book with me, *You'll See it When You Believe It*, by Wayne Dyer. Not wanting to be rude, I accepted the book even though I knew I couldn't read. But then, maybe if I believed I could, I could.

Surprise, I read it. Not easily. Not speedily, but I read it.

The same friend lent me *I'm OK-You're OK*. If I could read by believing I could, maybe I wasn't a loner either. Perhaps I'd just made that up, too. Just shy is all.

Seems trite, but true. Shifting my attitude changed my life.

ᐉ Magnetic Bedding ᐉ

It was through Lifespring that I met amazing people; some have become life-long friends. In 1987, I left the car phone business and joined a Lifespring friend in a unique multi-level company, Japan Life International, selling high-end magnetic bedding.

I was intrigued with bio magnetics. Wanted to understand what I was selling. I studied magnetic healing methodology used in the East, read Davis and Rawls's *The Magnetic Blueprint of Life*, Becker and Selden's *The Body Electric: Electromagnetism and the Foundation of Life*, John Evans's *Mind, Body and Electromagnetism*, Richard Gerber's *Vibrational Medicine in the 21st Century*, and Larry Dossey's *Space Time and Medicine*.

I've kept all my books and have enjoyed going back to reviewing my highlighted passages. Recent images of sperm competing for entry into the egg and the egg's selection process suggest that magnetic forces may well be involved. Much was made then of the complexity and importance of an energy field that surrounds us. I wonder whether it is the same thing as the microbial cloud we carry around us. Much was made of energy flow within us, like the ordered magnetic frequencies up our spine and energy drops where we have illness or pain. We "New Agers" envisioned being in a shared flow of awareness. Contemporary thinkers are wondering whether our minds are located somewhere outside of our bodies.

In earlier times, humans received magnetic stimulation by living on or near the earth. In modern times, concrete floors and sidewalks, asphalt, high-rise apartments, rubber tires, etc. block or distort the earth's magnetic field. The point of magnetic bedding is to provide a stable magnetic environment for balancing our complex electrical activity during sleep, a time when our bodies heal and recharge.

The "Sleep System" included a two-inch-thick mattress-topper containing spaced lines of dipole magnets, 850 Gauss. (Gauss is a measure of strength. Dipole means that both a positive and a negative charge exist on each side of a flat magnet.) The system included a down comforter embedded with magnets, an optional secondary comforter to Velcro onto the first for colder climates, a firm pillow with magnets, a full set of cotton linens, and carrying cases. A travel-sized mat with linens and seat cushion were also available.

Sales were all in-home demonstrations that began with us (the salespeople) giving "roller massages" to our customers, a Japanese custom designed to thank the customer for letting us show our wares. We would place a single bed-sized magnetic mat on the floor; the customer would lie on it face down. Using a unique double-ball stick roller, we gave the customer a full back roll-out from neck to feet, about 15 minutes.

Then we showed them the feel and thickness of the down comforter. We showed swatches of bedding designs. We explained the benefits of using our sleep system.

Jo, my mentor, and I did well in Japan Life. We rose to the top rank of the sales force. In 1989, I was tapped to be a sales trainer. My territory was the Northeast, from Maine to North Carolina and inland to Philadelphia. I flew to four to six cities on each trip unless it snowed; then I was on a train.

I would be gone a month at a time, four times a year. With a shoulder strap, I carried a single-size magnetic mattress folded in thirds in a canvas carrying case: 35 pounds. In the other hand, I held a see-through carrying case containing a compressed comforter with linens and a massage roller, plus a light suitcase for myself. I was strong then but still visited my shiatsu massage therapist on the way home from the airport. At the gym, I began training for the Over-50 Women's Body Building Competition, which never happened because I pulled a plantar tendon being too rowdy in an aerobics class. Just readying myself was rewarding.

All this kept me away from home a lot, but the kids were busy. After high school, Anne enrolled in Lee Strasberg's Actors Studio to hone her acting skills. Yano was in high school. I had an in-home office, so Diane, my secretary, was at my house weekdays.

The company appreciated their sales force with monthly awards: certificates, plaques, and trophies. One year, they flew the top salespeople with a husband or wife to Japan for a week and treated us like royalty. Since I didn't have a spouse, the boss let me take Yano, then 16. We attended meetings, met other international sales folks and went sightseeing around Tokyo and surrounding rural areas.

One morning arriving for work at the Los Angeles office, we found our entry doors and windows crisscrossed with two-by-fours and "Keep Out" signs. Apparently, Japan Life was making "health claims" without proper authority, or something like that.

I know the health benefits are real. I had researched magnetics by reading books on magnetic healing, vibrational medicine, and alternative healing. I attended conferences and visited with Dr. Buryl Payne and other researchers.

Six of us had participated in an experiment that studied live-cell behavior comparing the blood of persons on and off the magnetic mattress. We performed Live Cell Analysis by taking a finger-stick drop of blood, placing in on a microscope slide, and applying a coverslip to spread the liquid evenly. Blood cells moved sluggishly and platelets clumped in samples from persons who had not used the mattress. When a person had been on a magnetic mattress for 30 minutes, we could see the red blood cells move freely and tumble over one another; the magnetic poles of both the magnets and the red blood cells attracted and repelled one another. The clumps of cells and platelets broke up as well.

Additionally, I heard many testimonials from sleep system users, mostly about restful sleep, diminished muscular aches and headaches. I had slept in my sleep system less than six months when the inflammation in my fingers from arthritis dissipated.

I knew and taught the benefits of magnetic healing, but proving it is like having to prove that love exists.

That was 30 years ago. I still sleep on my magnetic mattress pad and snuggle in with my magnetic comforter and magnetic pillow. So do the four Japan Life friends I stay in touch with.

∽ Social Life ∽

The '80s had been enjoyable. Caucasian magnetic bedding users were often "New Age" folks. Jo and I hung out with them as our customers came via word of mouth. The good vibes sunk in. We went to presentations at the Onion Church in North Hills to hear Darryl Anka channel Bashar. We went with the folks from *Meditation Magazine* up a pine mountain to hug trees, plant crystals at their roots by moonlight, and share breakfast at daybreak. We rollerskated the beach path from Santa Monica to Venice. Life was delightful.

∽ Street Vendor ∽

After the demise of Japan Life, I needed income. Anne had been selling seafood out of a truck fitted with two deep freezers and was tired of it, so I bought her truck and became a street vendor. On Thursdays, I went to the busy import market in downtown Los Angeles and filled up my freezers with packages of frozen shrimp, scallops, blue crab meat, and fillets.

Around 3 a.m. on Friday mornings, I loaded the truck and headed up the highway to claim a roadside spot before dawn. A favorite was on Highway 126 north of Los Angeles. I could come home every night.

State Road 58 west of Bakersfield going toward the ocean was another favorite place. I traveled with a cooler full of food for me for the weekend: tuna salad, sandwiches, apples, cookies, juice, coffee, and water. I arrived by sunup, sold all day, would break down about 5 p.m. and go to a Motel 6 where I had made reservations. After sleep, I'd be out early on Saturday and again on Sunday.

My favorite spot was up in the mountain, past Joshua Tree National Park to Twenty-Nine Palms, then north to the Air-Ground Task Forces Training Command, a military base. Every other Friday was pay-day there; at 5 p.m., the base gates would open and here they came, galloping to see what I had brought them. One homesick young recruit would shed a tear of joy and give me a tip when I could get him blue crab from Maryland.

No matter where I went, I came home via Interstate 5. I always stopped at the Jack-in-the-Box at the top of the last hill to pick up a burger for a homeless guy who lived under the freeway bridge at Nordhoff Street near my house. He was always waiting for me, said "Thanks," and meant it.

When one of my freezers gave out, I switched to selling Blue Block Sunglasses: 25 dollars for a box of 25 at the downtown market, selling them on the road for 5 dollars each. No point going to the military base anymore. Sad.

∽ Herbalife ∽

At the same time I was a street vendor, I was trying to sell Herbalife vitamin and supplement products during the week. Not good. I had to buy and store a lot of product. I had to attend training sessions. The nutrition claims were weak at best. I used the product myself and didn't experience any benefits. Neither did customers. I wound up giving away a lot of pills.

∽ HealthRider ∽

A Herbalife acquaintance talked me into marketing the HealthRider, a pioneering home-exercise machine. It was a cross between rowing and a stationary bike. I got one to demo and showed it at the Whole Life Expo, but alas, no buyers.

In 1992, my truck gave out, my street-vendor enthusiasm gave out, and Yano, now 19, graduated and moved out to share a house with three others in Reseda, not far away. He had a good job at Solley's famous deli in Sherman Oaks. Anne, now 27, was on her own most of the time, but coming back to live at the house on occasion. I was the only one left in the big, old home with lots of upkeep.

It was time to move on. I was now 60.

Chapter 25: Next Venture

Beth said, "Mom, you need to get out of LA. Too expensive, too much traffic, and you have no friends there." Right. "Why don't you come back to Gainesville? Lots going on here, and you'd fit right into a college town." Right. I'd lived in California for 20 years.

I put the house up for sale and got busy giving things away and throwing things out. When the house sold, I sold my Sapphire Blue 1979 Toyota Supra that had 250,000 miles on it but was still in good shape. I called in the Salvation Army to haul off what was left, hired a moving van, and flew with my cat, Missy, to Jacksonville, Florida, where Beth and her partner, Barbara, met me with hugs and smiles. We drove south where they lived on Lake Melrose, stopping by Betty's Pizza on the way.

When the moving van arrived, I had them put everything in storage while I looked for a home nearby. Right in Melrose, I found a charming cracker house (a style of wood-frame home, a favorite in the 19th century in Florida characterized by metal roofs, raised floors, and large porches.) It had two bedrooms, one bath, a large kitchen, and a fireplace in the living room. Just my size. On the south side, a garage had been fashioned from an old carriage house. The sizable tree-bordered yard swept down to a depression that filled when it rained, summoning hundreds of tiny frogs to croak their love songs with gusto.

One day when I needed to go into Gainesville, 20 miles west, I borrowed Beth's Toyota truck. I couldn't believe how friendly everyone was, waving, smiling, saying, "Hi," everywhere I went. I told Beth about it. She laughed. "Mom, I have peace signs, an equal rights sticker, and rainbow flags all over my truck. Those were my friends welcoming you."

What a joy having ready-made friends who were always willing to give me a hand.

A small, computerized sign business was advertised for sale in the local paper. Interesting. It could fit into my second bedroom with a long worktable. I met the owners: Charlie and Jake, two gay graduate students who were finishing at the University of Florida. I bought the business complete with a customer list, equipment, and supplies. They helped me set everything up at my house and trained me.

I bought a used panel truck and lettered it with the C&J Signs logo on three sides. I turned my garage into a workshop where I built and painted larger sign structures.

C&J Signs was clearly a two-person business. I asked around and learned of a woman named Lynn who taught crafts to Girl Scouts. I found her, pitched/begged her, and she said, "OK." We got busy as we had two customers waiting.

We designed signs on the computer with special software, then send it on to a cutting machine that cut the design onto a sheet of vinyl. Lynn worked the design and cutting phases, we both did "weeding" (removing unwanted vinyl after cutting), and I went out to the customers to install the prepared vinyl signs. They can be attached to a variety of surfaces such as yard signs, lettering on cars, trucks, windshields, magnetic signs, banners of all sizes, four-by-eight wood signs mounted on four-by-four posts, notebooks, duffle bags, street signs, and more.

Early weekday mornings, I drove a half-hour into Gainesville to the Health and Fitness Center, took a 7 a.m. aerobics class, and was back in Melrose to open shop by 9. A rush, but invigorating. One morning, I came into the classroom to find people getting ready for yoga. Oh, NO! Change of schedule. Aerobics was now at 8.

After grumbling for a bit, I decided that since I was there, I might as well take a dumb yoga class. The teacher put me in the back of the room so I could watch and learn—a good thing because I could hardly do any of those poses. I must have looked like the Tin Woodswoman. Downright embarrassing. But I was hooked. I love a challenge and don't mind failing.

Life in Melrose was laid-back, relaxing. The town was an hour and a half from the Atlantic Ocean and an hour and a half from the Gulf of Mexico. We'd go beaching now and then. There also were rivers, lakes, and natural springs. Festivals and events occurred weekly. In Gainesville, there were more events going on than one could attend.

I was happily settling in when a miracle happened.

Beth's partner, Barbara, was a Medical Consultant teaching doctors about the latest echo sonography (ultrasound) technology and equipment. After her seminar one day, a doctor, Dr. Schneider, asked Barbara if she would come to his clinic in Coffeeville, Kansas, for a couple of weeks to teach his staff how to use the ultrasound equipment he'd just bought. She did. Then he asked her if she would join his team. "If the price is right," she said. She was getting tired of traveling.

"I can make it right," he responded.

"And if I can bring my partner, Beth. She's a carpenter."

"I can do that," he said. "I have lots of work to be done on my place." His place was a mini-ranch just outside of town. So Beth and Barb took off for Kansas, leaving me behind in Melrose. I made signs, planted vegetables, and talked to locals and frogs for a couple of months. Then it happened.

Barbara told Dr. Schneider, "You know, you could use a nutritionist on staff here."

"I know," he said. "I'm a health nut myself and try to get my patients on the latest diet."

"Well, Beth's mother is a professional nutritionist, and she just retired. She might be willing to help you out."

Dr. Schneider called me; we talked. There it was: my dream come true, a chance to return to my true love, foods and nutrition and a comfortable salary. I easily sold my little cracker house with its stocked workshop. I sold C&J Signs with the van, computers, worktable, supplies, and customer list for a nice profit and moved to Coffeyville, Kansas, with Missy, my cat.

That was 1995. I was 63.

Changing Times

Chapter 26: Back to Nutrition

As I hung up from talking with Dr. Schneider, I realized in a panic that I hadn't been paying attention to food and nutrition for a long time. Suspecting that I was probably ill-prepared, I sent for a battery of textbooks for courses required for an advanced degree in Nutrition.

This was three years before the invention of Google.

The primary textbook they sent was *Understanding Normal and Clinical Nutrition*, 1994 edition, by Whitney, Cataldo, and Rolfes, 981 pages not counting an Appendix, Tables, Index, and listings for over 180 diets, all associated with medical conditions. The trouble was, it didn't mention the modern diets that I was sure Dr. Schneider wanted for his patients. Neither did any of the other books they sent.

I still have and refer to Understanding Normal and Clinical Nutrition, *useful basic information.*

I'd heard of the Atkins Diet, the Pritikin Diet, and knew there were weight-loss diets and clinics. Rather than getting worried, I decided to ask Dr. Schneider what diet he was using now and if he'd let me read his resource material.

Except for Ohio, I'd never been in the Midwest. Coffeyville is on the Verdigris River in the southeast corner of the state, beautiful open country, green with rolling hills, cows, and horses. Once a center of industry and manufacturing, it was now quiet due to industry changes. But it was famous as the home of the final shoot-out of the Dalton Gang on October 5, 1892.

The clinic was surprisingly spacious, well-staffed, and offered most lab work done on site. Dr. Schneider gave me an office and introduced me around. He was recommending Barry Sears's Zone Diet. Not bad. I could do that.

I bunked with Beth and Barbara while looking for a place to live. They lived in one of Dr. Schneider's mobile homes on his mini-ranch. I decided to rent since I didn't feel like I'd be there forever. I found a suitable house up the road in Independence, furnished it from the second-hand store, and settled in. The first week there, a neighborhood dog gruesomely tore Missy into pieces. I was devastated. She was 13, a kitten we'd saved from the house fire in 1982.

My job at the clinic was to accompany the doctor as he visited with patients and schedule them for a consultation with me so I could to talk to them about the new Zone Diet, get them set up with the necessary dietary changes, and then follow through. Since they were in my office for a half-hour, I had time to talk with them about basic nutrition.

Each patient and I would complete my four-page questionnaire about their eating history and habits. I'd get an idea of their food knowledge by giving them a list of 10 foods and ask whether each was a carbohydrate food, a protein food, or a fat food. Interesting. Broccoli often came up as a protein food. Why? "Because it's good for you." Most of their food and nutrition knowledge had been gleaned watching television.

Many patients were farming families with home-grown, home-cooked food, and were eating healthy already.

When Dr. Schneider learned that I had taken yoga classes, he wanted me to teach yoga to him and his wife. They had a small gym in their house. We were all awkward at this since I had no teacher-training and they didn't know yoga at all, but we enjoyed stretching to soft music. Next thing I knew, news of our private yoga class was in the local newspaper. I was asked to hold a class for local homemakers. Six of them met with me in the Episcopal Church twice a week. That led to my writing a monthly column in the local paper. I was getting busy.

The next year, Dr. Schneider switched his patients to the latest new diet even though most of our patients were doing well on their Zone-based diets. He took his entire professional staff to the ACAM meeting in California to learn about Dr. Peter D'Adamo's *Eat Right for Your Type* diet. (ACAM, the American College for Advancement in Medicine, is a not-for-profit, membership-based association of integrative medicine physicians.)

I understood the premise of this diet, but reducing it to "blood type" and then further to personality type didn't feel right. Dr. D'Adamo spoke at length about his research on body fluids in general, inferring that blood type would fall into line. I investigated his work later and found no research to substantiate that idea, but there were no contraindications either.

I spoke with Dr. Schneider about offering customized diets for his patients. Farm families didn't need a diet, and, sometimes that latest popular diet wasn't right for a particular patient.

The doc gave me a curious look. Then explained how his business worked—the "bottom line." Bringing the latest diet onboard each year kept his business profitable and the patients trusting that he was keeping up with science.

He said if I had a problem with that, I might better find another "position."

໙ The New Nutrition ໙

Something deeper was troubling me. It seemed that the field of nutrition had changed in attitude and approach in the 25 years since I had been active in the profession. Perhaps it was I who was out of step, not Dr. Schneider. Food, nutrition, and diet seemed less about the health of the person or patient than it once was, more focused on products, not people.

I saw the change all around me. Nutrition was no longer about foods from the garden and pastures that we brought into our kitchens and cooked in time-honored ways to nourish our bodies. It wasn't about chewing food so the saliva could mix in to start the process, nor about the role and function of the stomach, intestines, and absorption. It wasn't about the many pathways to the organs and how that worked, down to the cells. It wasn't about the importance of balancing the food intake and synergism, how it all works together. It wasn't about the many factors that affect the utilization of food. Nor did this new nutrition concern itself with how food preparation affects the nutritional value and our metabolism.

It was about packaged foods in the supermarkets, fast-food, restaurant food, and snacks. About diets. About saving time, making meals easy and mobile. Food companies were advertising heavily in magazines and TV, offering a dizzying array of unrecognizable instant dinners and treats. And bread that lasted for a month on the counter without getting moldy.

Never mind all that. I'd resist the trend. Surely, I would find a situation that still honored old-school practices.

Jobs of any kind were scarce as hen's teeth in rural Kansas. I expanded my search. I landed an interview at the Jane Phillips Hospital Medical Complex in Bartlesville, Oklahoma, 30 miles south of Coffeyville.

"No," said my interviewer. "We don't need a nutritionist, but can you teach exercise?"

"Yes," I said with confidence, recalling the Jane Fonda-type classes that I had taken back in California. I figured I could fake it 'til I made it.

"You're hired."

And so it was that I changed careers, but not much and not willingly. I'd figure something out.

I rented an old, single-wide trailer home on 43 acres on the Salt River in Okesa, 10 miles west of Bartlesville. Okesa's population was 14 families, spaced far apart. Historically, Okesa was a rest stop on the Shawnee Trail, a longhorn cattle-drive route from Texas to railroad trailheads in Kansas. An old saloon now housed a general store and eatery. The family who owned the former 12-grade schoolhouse offered its subterranean gym as a community social gathering place and a safe-haven during tornado season.

It was 1997 with Y2K fear that computer systems might crash at midnight Year 2000. This might be a good time to play "Little House on the Prairie," I thought. Be self-sufficient.

It was late summer. I put in a 35-foot by 10-foot straw-bale garden as there was less than a quarter-inch of topsoil. I filled the garden with barn waste from a local dairy, grass clippings, lots of leaves, and bottom sand and mud from the Salt River. I turned the whole mess under and over many times with a potato fork and let it sit over winter.

My garden was big enough to feed myself and to barter for milk and butter. I ordered heritage vegetable seeds to build a traditional food

supply. I planted a variety of heritage sunflower seeds to decorate the front of my trailer with smiles.

This was a very opportune time to try vegetarianism, the milder Lacto-Ovo kind that permits dairy and eggs.

Using hand tools and traditional ways, I ground local organic wheat and baked Gramma's recipes for bread and yeast rolls. I sun-dried herbs, fruits, and vegetables. I tried grinding soybeans for tofu and soy milk, but soybeans were so hard they broke my grinder.

I used oil lamps for light, solar cooking when possible.

An orange feral cat came to my trailer at night for food I'd leave on the porch. One day, she didn't show up. A few days later, I heard faint meowing under my trailer, crawled under and found two tiny kittens, one orange, one deep gray. I called them "Orange" and "Smokey." Not very creative. It was comforting to have warm little bodies to pet and talk to.

I learned the exercise routines for cardio and pulmonary rehab patients from the previous exercise teacher and took over her classes. Then I took a mail-order course in Personal Fitness Training, earning certification. I solicited my cardio and pulmonary rehab class participants to continue their workouts with me in their homes upon their release. They liked to chat about food while we exercised. They welcomed my knowledge and appreciated my "customized" recommendations.

I got back into weight training at the Bartlesville Fitness Center. A flyer was posted there one day for Ayer Yoga teacher training near Oklahoma City. Ayer Yoga is based on Ayurveda healing by balancing the three doshas, Vata, Pitta, and Kapha, and eating a vegetarian diet.

Here was an opportunity to become a certified yoga teacher.

I went to the training: 30 days at the ashram with about 20 others studying how yoga asanas (poses) affect various body functions. We learned how to move into, maintain, and release each asana, then flow to the next. We studied the history of yoga and the basics of anatomy, physiology, and kinesiology. We learned about meridians (pathways in the body along which vital energy flows) and pranayama (the regulation of the breath through specific techniques and exercises.)

Days began at dawn with meditation and ended at 5 p.m. with a beautiful spread of vegetarian food cooked for us by a Buddhist chef. We practiced quiet, mindful eating in which every bite is precious, *shojin ryori ("devotion cuisine")*.

Close to the end of the training, we started our day at 5 a.m., still dark, with a practice session outdoors in four inches of new-fallen snow. Barefoot. No one said a word, of course, nor even looked at one another. I went into a silent panic, certain my feet would freeze. During the beginning meditation, I focused on warm feet. By the end of the practice, an hour, my feet weren't exactly warm, but they weren't frozen either. It was a test. We all passed.

After the 30-day training in the ashram, I went back to Okesa, but the training wasn't over.

Next, we were to perform dharma, the giving of yoga to others. I volunteered to teach yoga to the cheerleaders at Pawhuska High School, 30 miles west of Okesa.

Pawhuska High School Cheerleaders

The final step in training was to return to Oklahoma City for 30 additional days to complete the requirements for Yoga 200 Certification with Yoga Alliance.

Although I was enjoying my new teaching career, old-school nutrition was on my mind. I bristled at this "new nutrition." It seemed wrong. Fortunately, not all nutritionists were on board with these changes. "Integrative" and "Complementary" medicine was growing, which made it easier to offer and compare both traditional and contemporary food and nutrition options.

Andrew Weil's new book, *Spontaneous Healing*, spoke to my passion as it offered a step-by-step plan for natural healing, including nutrition. I contacted his organization and got permission to offer a workshop. They sent me 25 small pamphlets: "Dr. Weil's 8-Week Plan for Optimal Healing Power" with an 8-week action plan including weekly projects, diet tips with recipes, supplements, exercise, and mental/spiritual activities.

I advertised around town; 20 women showed up for the workshop. At the onset, we reviewed the agenda, asked and answered questions, and got underway with Week 1. We met each week to share and discuss. The eighth week ended with a potluck. Each participant made and brought a healthy dish they had never tried before the workshop. Fun.

One of the attendees was Billie, owner of Bartlesville's Health Food Shop. Her business offered a rich variety of health foods of the day and a goodly array of supplements. I learned from her about supplements. Billie was one of my first yoga students.

I started giving yoga classes at the YWCA. The turn-out might have been bigger were it not for many husbands refusing to let their wives participate due to religious beliefs that yoga was a subversive oriental religion designed to lead Christians astray. (Yoga is not a religion. Simply stated, it blends controlled breathing, body positions, and meditation to create a state of insight and tranquility.)

I moved the class to the YMCA. Health-minded folks. There I built a large class including two men: a fireman and a construction worker.

I continued giving talks around town about Natural Nutrition, passing out "Caroline's Recipe for Wellness" based on Dr. Weil's teachings.

To this day, I still give it out, updating it every so often. See Appendix 5.

Y2K came and went. Good thing. I couldn't make the self-sufficiency thing work. It was unbelievably hard work and time-consuming, so I gave it up. My vegetarian diet wasn't working either. My belly stayed bloated, and my mind was spacey. Not right for me.

Instead, I made new friends, joined a book club, got a computer, hooked up to the internet. What a blessing! For the first time in my life, I could access information right from my home, and lots of it. Answers to so many mysteries were at my fingertips. Now I could follow the facts, fiction, fads, and trends in food and nutrition.

Indeed, there was nonsense going on.

Like bad-mouthing eggs. I'd brushed that off because it was dumb. Eggs have been eaten since the beginning of human time and revered as "nature's most perfect food."

Like bad-mouthing real milk. Traditionally, milk is just food that is produced by mammals to feed their young, including humans. Pasteurizing milk was developed in the early 1900s for sterility in medical practice. When safe non-pasteurized milk was tested and marketed, it was called Certified Milk.

During WWII, the armed services sent pasteurized milk to our troops overseas because of its long shelf-life. After the war, pasteurized milk quietly became "milk" implying that it had all the nutritional benefits of traditional milk, which it doesn't. Certified milk became "raw milk" suggesting that it was dangerous, which it isn't.

The war on butter was and is still going strong, ever since post-WWII days, always being demonized with pseudo-science and slick advertising. At the Food and Flavor Lab at ADL, we were unable to create butter flavor or the sensory feel of "mouth bloom." There is still something magical about butter.

I tried to stay focused and catch up with the food and nutrition of the day.

But I sensed that profound changes had been taking place, foreshadowing a very different future for wellness.

Chapter 27: Cultural Shift

Traditionally, food is what people foraged, grew, raised, caught, and ate to satisfy their hunger and sustain their lives.

Over time, that definition broadened to include: nutritious substances that are eaten or absorbed by humans, animals, and plants to support life.

In the 1900s, we became more sophisticated, understanding that food is material, usually from plants or animals, that contains carbohydrates, fats, proteins, vitamins, or minerals, and produces energy, stimulates growth and maintains life.

Sometime in the '30s, food production began to change due to new agricultural practices. The vocabulary started to change, too.

Traditional farming, with its long history of tending and nurturing soil with natural fertilizers, alternating crops, and enriching the soil with nitrogen-forming cover crops, got a new name: "Organic Farming."

"Conventional Farming" became the term for industrial agriculture. To increase yields, farmers fed their crops chemical fertilizer called N-P-K (Nitrogen-Phosphorus-Potassium). It worked great. Higher yield = more money for the farmers, more food for the consumers and a healthy chemical fertilizer business for investors. Agribusiness escalated with one-crop farms using heavy equipment.

After a few decades, industrial crops began to show signs of ill health. The weakened plants attracted pests. Consumers noticed their food didn't taste as good as it once had.

Scientists determined that after years of feeding only N-P-K, the plants had progressively sucked up all the other nutrients from the soil that they needed for healthy growth.

Rather than trying to replace the missing soil nutrients, a simple solution emerged. A Swiss chemist, Paul Hermann Muller, discovered that a new pesticide called DDT designed to kill malaria-carrying mosquitos could also destroy the pesky bugs that had invaded our conventional food crops[2].

Because I gardened, I had followed *Rodale's* magazine and *Encyclopedia of Organic Gardening* book. I'd read Helen and Scott Nearing's *Living the Good Life* and Rachel Carson's *Silent Spring*, which documented the negative impact of agricultural chemicals and pesticides. Not everyone agreed: Big Food railed against this idea, but organic devotees took action. DDT was killing birds, animals, and people, too. With robust response, DDT was banned in 1972.

I'd followed the efforts of Cesar Chavez to improve the condition of farmworkers and participated in the grape boycott and cheered in 1979 with the signing of the California Organic Food Act. By 2000, legislation and certification standards were finally enacted. Reclamation of the soil began with the resurgence of organic (traditional) farming practices. The sweetness of real food lingered on because of the persistent efforts of the organic food movement.

By the 1980s, we had learned the names of dozens of nutrients and the roles they played in our quest for good health. Food stopped being the kind of thing you could see, cook, and eat. Instead, food was defined by its nutrients. What a boon for the food and medical industries! Now they can shift their focus from selling food to selling nutrients. There are tens of thousands of nutrients, each of which can probably be related to health in some way or another. Good for business.

Simultaneously, the word "health" seemed to be shifting to mean "avoiding sickness." Health Fairs were about sickness; media was about sickness. All people talked about was what was wrong with them or their spouses, kids, or pets. When I was growing up, we were taught that talking about sickness was bad manners.

Advertising introduced consumers to scientific-sounding words. People were inundated with facts and figures, implying that it was now the customer's job to take care of their health. More accurately, it was the woman's job to take care of everyone's health. The food industry was busy doing man's work: making money. That's what industry does. It is beholden to the shareholders.

While consumers were learning this new nutrition vocabulary from TV and magazines, newspapers and their doctors, and were busy eating their nutrients, the definition of food had changed, quietly.

---

[2] *See "The Future of Food" video, Appendix 7*

The Food and Drug Administration had changed its definition of food to this: "(1) articles used for food or drink for man or other animals, (2) chewing gum, and (3) articles used for components of any such article."

This loose definition of food opened the floodgates for processed food and gave great power to the food industry. The FDA had openly shifted its allegiance from the consumer to "cooperating with" and "in support of" of the food industry.

Nutrients for Dinner

Do you remember when we talked about meals like this?

"Hi Becky, What did you have for dinner?"

"Fried Chicken." End of subject.

In the 1990s, Becky would more likely have said proudly, out loud or to herself:

"Well, for my protein, I had a small piece of chicken, not very much, mind you, about 3 ounces, just the size of my palm, lightly sautéed in a tablespoon of Olestra. I hardly ever eat meat, but every so often I do. I think a little won't hurt you. And a small potato with just a spoon of sour cream and chives. Chives are a vegetable, but since there weren't very many, I guess they don't count. But I did have broccoli, three flowerets, lightly steamed to retain all the vitamins and antioxidants. Without salt. Watching my sodium, you know. And, of course, I always have a salad: romaine, it has the most B vitamins. I put in half a small tomato, a few slices of cucumber, a little virgin olive oil, cold-pressed, and a squeeze of lemon. Since I had only four vegetables, I opted for a fresh fruit compote for dessert. A little fruit keeps you regular. It's got fiber. Came with a wee dollop of whipped cream. Have to splurge sometimes. Could have been Cool Whip. Oh, and I always have water to drink, spring water, with a twist of lemon.

The whole thing came to under 750 calories. Not bad, Huh?"

Lobbying and special interest groups proliferated. Industry personnel got government watchdog positions. Government employees moved into industry. Industry interests fought for control of the government's Food Pyramids and for industry-sponsored education and research. Advertising to children was untethered. Nefarious activities to gain and hold control over food and nutrition were in full swing.

The battle over supplements is an example. The food market had exploded, the flavor had been beefed up with natural and artificial flavorings, but there was a suspicion that the actual food nutrients lost with Conventional Farming had never been replaced.

Food scientists suggested they provide the missing nutrients directly to the customer. The supplement industry was born.

Initially, these lab-made supplements weren't utilized well by the human body. Micronizing the ingredients didn't work either. Then food chemists chelated (attached) their chemical nutrients to organic molecules that the human body usually consumes. That worked. The supplement business bloomed, promising a bevy of benefits.

In the early '90s, the pharmaceutical industry felt the competition and demanded that supplements be regulated as drugs, which would have required extensive testing and government oversight. The supplement companies got busy rallying farmers, businesses, and customers to petition the FDA to classify supplements as food.

Amazingly, it worked, resulting in "The Dietary Supplement Health and Education Act of 1994" (DSHEA). Under this act, supplements are mainly unregulated, without proof of effectiveness or safety needed to market the products. The FDA intervenes only in cases of significant consumer complaints or mislabeling.

Business boomed. Food supplements, herbal remedies, a bevy of new products designed to solve every manner of malady and desire popped up everywhere. Man-made wonders, freeze-dried berries and roots from a remote island in pills and powders, drinks and shakes, all brought joy to the happy, health-seeking customer.

I got busy reading. The Bartlesville Book Store would send away for books on lend. I read Joan Dye Gussow's *The Feeding Web*, Dr. Elson Haas's *Staying Healthy with Nutrition, Eating with the Seasons,* and *The Detox Book*, Dr. Deepak Chopra's *Quantum Healing* and *Ageless Body Timeless Mind*, and Andrew Weil's *Eating Well for Optimum Health*. All were about real, natural nutrition. The bookstore folks could not find any books about the current industry-government tug of war.

Scientific-sounding diets were being popularized. The Zone Diet, the Eat Right for Your Type, Atkins, Dean Ornish, Pritikin, Sugar Busters, Juice Fasting and Detoxification, Vegetarian, and the Raw Foods diets. There were lists of foods that one should and shouldn't eat, what was good and what was bad for you. Doctors, too busy or not knowledgeable about foods and nutrition, were educated by industry and became spokespersons for these trends.

Competition exploded. Everybody jumped into the game.

I laugh when I remember an irritated patient asking me, "Why can't you nutritionists make up your minds?" Even the experts were opinionated. Confused maybe? Offering a variety of explanations, claims, beliefs. This situation quickly led to the emergence of self-appointed experts, many of whom weren't nutritionists, dietitians, or had ever cooked or gardened.

Everything was moving so fast that True experts were scarce, and the demand was high. A bona fide expert is a person who has knowledge about and experience in the field of his or her claimed expertise. This wasn't happening. Merely adding a couple of capital letters behind one's name does not make that someone an expert. A PhD in psychology is NOT an expert in nutrition. An MD is NOT educated or trained in nutrition. No one is an expert on aging. Writing a book, making a DVD, or preaching to a paid audience on Public Television does not qualify one as an expert. Not even being a celebrity makes one an expert.

I began to notice that no one knew THE answers. I mean factually. Not even the experts. And how could they? Experts are expected to know answers to incredibly complex problems. There are infinite possibilities. Over 5 billion people were on the planet in 1990, every one of them with unique needs depending on gender, age, health, heredity, and lifestyle. The best that a food and nutrition expert can do is narrow down the probabilities based on his or her knowledge and experience.

And intention. A certified expert will walk their talk and have nothing to sell.

Never mind! No time for details. The food industry is busy selling FDA-approved food, the stuff people will put in their mouths and swallow.

And then the bookstore folks found Warren J. Belasco's *Appetite for Change: How the Counterculture Took on the Food Industry*. There it was! Finally, a treatise on the New Nutrition. Food for profit. Not health. I devoured it with a new understanding of what had happened since I left my profession to be a good wife and how natural nutrition fit into the picture. Or didn't.

For me, offering the most reasonable eating plan for a particular client or group of like-minded folks to support optimum health is still my goal. At a minimum, that means sticking to foods from nature, as they have a solid track record. Industrial foods are unknowns.

It was dawning on me that professionalism as I'd always known it was not held in high regard in this new world of industrial food and nutrition. Traditional organic food was fighting for its life against a foe that had no scruples.

* * *

The more I learned, the more frustrated I became, lost in the BS. The sheer magnitude of the damage done to the field of Foods and Nutrition was heartbreaking: the dearth of factual knowledge, the presence of spin doctors, the strong-arm of industry and their willingness to deceive and their lack of compassion. There was corrosion of trust. The absence of basic health knowledge overall was overwhelming.

The role of the nutritionist had been relegated to the biochemistry and metabolism of food and nutrition, especially their components. Dietitians had organized and moved up from taking orders from doctors to being spokespersons for the food industry.

I didn't see how I could fit into the current state of foods and nutrition. Glitzy advertising pushed the latest nutrient or diet. I just couldn't do that. My credentials for a research position were out of date. I was out of date. Now 66. Maybe just give up my dream of returning to nutrition. Hang around here. Teach yoga. Tend my garden. Enjoy the book club. Pet my cats. It's a pretty good life.

* * *

As if foreordained, I received two phone calls from Las Vegas on the same day.

Call one: Yano's voice. "Hi, Mom. I'm OK but, well, things aren't going well. I haven't seen my son in a long time. I'm wondering if you would come for a visit and maybe lend a hand."

Call two: "Is this Jovanni's gramma?" A young woman's voice.

"Yes, it is."

"This is Suzie, a friend of Jasmine's, (Jovanni's Mom). We found Jovanni by himself in Paradise Park five blocks from his apartment. We're worried that Protective Services might pick him up."

Jovanni: 4½ years old. My only grandchild.

"Is Jasmine all right?"

"Not really."

"Thank you for letting me know. I'll fly out right away."

Shifting Focus

Chapter 28: Gramma in Vegas

Jasmine's voice was welcoming when I called to ask if I could come for the weekend. The Tulsa to Las Vegas Weekend Vacation Package had a standby seat with a cheap room booked for two nights at the Golden Nugget. The plane ride was a party with balloons, booze, and a DJ. Everyone was excited to be going to Vegas. I managed to be congenial.

I rented a car and made it to Jasmine's apartment by late afternoon. She was in good spirits. Friends of hers were there. We exchanged pleasantries and ordered in pizza. Jovanni was shy, off by himself. Plans were made for me to pick him up early the next morning to visit Dad, an hour's drive away.

When I arrived, Jovanni was sitting on the curb out front, waiting for me. Yano was waiting when we got there. Excited to see one another, the boys goofed around. Guy things. Plus hugs and kisses. Yano and I talked about their family situation. It was a good day.

That evening, Jasmine told me how difficult it was for her to hold a job and take care of Jovanni, that she couldn't make enough to put him in daycare, that her friends couldn't help much as they were struggling, too. I noticed her nearly bare refrigerator, only Froot Loops in the cupboard.

Sunday morning, Jovanni and I went to the playground; my plane left early afternoon. Pale and thin, he had trouble climbing the monkey bars. That did it. I would move to Vegas. Help out. I had Social Security and was pretty good at finding jobs. I'd make it work. I couldn't bear the idea that my grandson would be raised by Social Services.

The return flight to Tulsa was full of sad, tired, hung-over, and broke passengers. Reliving the weekend, I fit right in.

It took a couple months for me to disengage from teaching exercise classes, yoga, personal fitness clients, and friends in Bartlesville, Pawhuska, and Okesa. They all came together to give me a lovely going-away party. Many came by my garden to take plants they could use. I found a home for Orange and Smokey with a friend who needed mousers. I packed my things. Beth came to help and drive. We stuffed a U-Haul, hooked up my car, and I took off for Vegas, arriving at sundown on Halloween, 2001.

The Vegas Valley is dry, dusty, and decorated with rocks and a few scrawny bushes, a stark reversal from green Okesa. With persistence, I found a small second-floor apartment with a bit of green: a balcony facing a tree and the bedroom window overlooking a golf course. It was in Henderson, a mere mile from Jasmine's place in Vegas.

Life was chaotic as Jasmine worked a variety of jobs at varying hours (Vegas is a "24-hour town"). Jovanni was now in half-day kindergarten, and I was filling in as substitute Mom, whenever. In summer, Jovanni was in "summer camp," and I got busy looking for a morning job.

Life got even more chaotic when I realized that food-related jobs were in restaurants or in hospitals—jobs like cooking or serving. No thanks. I would find a job teaching fitness. Turns out, that was a problem too. The gyms were hiring only gorgeous YOUNG teachers. I was a dinosaur.

I found and joined a women's weekly breakfast group in which members look for and give job leads to other members. Through them, I learned that there was an opening for a personal fitness trainer at a large, upscale retirement community a half-hour "up the hill" from my place. I jumped on it, but no, they had just filled the position. I suggested they let me build an "in-home" fitness clientele for retirees who couldn't make it to the gym.

After a month, they said "OK." I put up flyers and set up booths at their Health Fairs and other events. I got a couple clients. I also got on the "sub-list" to teach classes for teachers who might need some time off. One of the residents helped me get a seated exercise class going that fit the needs of some. I did house-sitting. Within a year, I had a bit of income and morning work that didn't interfere with being a useful gramma.

However, a gramma has no rights on behalf of a grandchild in Nevada. I couldn't even get Jovanni a library card, much less handle an illness, accident, or school issues. We saw Yano most weekends but saw less and less of Jasmine. It was obvious what I needed to do. With pro bono effort and a lot of paperwork, I was awarded guardianship in October 2002. By spring, I was accepted into Nevada's Kinship Caretaker Program and had a bigger apartment.

There was another problem: finding food. Real food. Fresh organic food. Local, seasonal food. What did I expect? The Vegas Valley is a desert. Most of my life I'd eaten from a garden, fed my family from a garden, fresh and home-canned or frozen, from a butcher shop, a dairy, backyard chickens. My brain went into overtime.

I found a Whole Foods. But what wasn't in boxes, cans, or frozen came "fresh" from somewhere else. Or lovely greens that were bagged in polyphenol oxidase and wilted then spoiled as soon as the bag was opened. Their beautiful organic meat was out of my budget.

Fitness instructors net just over minimum wage after the costs of local, state, and federal licensing, business insurance, yearly CEU (Continuing Education Units) and CPR (cardiopulmonary resuscitation) requirements, transportation expenses, proper shoes, expected appropriate attire. Not to mention state, county, and local sales taxes. How about the years we spent in college and specialty schools and training to earn our certifications? What's the justification? "They teach because they love it, not for the pay." They are women.

Again, I had to take a step back from what I wanted to what I could afford. Jovanni and I ate lots of homemade mac and cheese, egg dishes, canned tuna casseroles, and SPAM diced and mixed into Rice-a-Roni. Memories of The Depression years. Thank goodness for potatoes, onions, and cabbage.

Cruising the web, I soon found a local farmer's market that brought produce into Henderson weekly from the Fresno, California valley. Yum. So tasty. Later, I learned about a CSA (Consumer Supported Agriculture) north of Vegas that made deliveries into Henderson. Garden grown veggies, fruits, berries, herbs, and flowers. I signed up for a small biweekly delivery.

Through them, I learned of a group of locals who ordered bulk deliveries of butchered Berkshire hogs from family farms way up in Utah. I bought a small top-loading freezer from Sears and signed up.

But fresh dairy? That was a big problem. Raw milk is illegal in Nevada; can't buy, sell, or transport fresh, natural dairy products. State-wide grassroots groups petitioned for legalization, but even after meeting all the requirements over two years, Governor Sandoval vetoed it. Why? Because he deemed it his responsibility to protect his residents from illness and possibly death. Same old BS.

Some people are lactose intolerant, some are allergic, but no one has ever died from consuming fresh, clean, properly processed and inspected raw milk.

I chose to be a law-breaker. No one, absolutely no one is going to tell me what I must feed or cannot feed myself and my family. I found several "underground milk runs." All hush-hush. No names. I joined one that ran up through Utah and over to Arizona where raw milk is legal. Deliveries were made at undisclosed locations at specific times. (No, I'm not going to tell you more.) I could buy gallons of fresh raw milk, raw cream, various cheeses, and butter.

When Arizona made that dairy farm move from its public land location, they went to Utah where there were other issues. I could only buy milk and cream, which I did and made my own butter. Delicious, but too time-consuming. So, I began traveling down to California buying six pounds of butter at a time and put them in my new freezer. That would last us six months. Why would I do that? Because butter from cows pastured on organic and wild grasses is one of the most concentrated sources of essential fat/oil-based nutrients in the world. I'm worth it. So is Jovanni.

But I digress.

Raising a grandchild has its challenges, especially one who is three generations younger. I got to learn a lot of new "stuff." So did Jovanni. We found mutual interest in museums, music, science documentaries, and

physical fitness. Jovanni eagerly participated in many sports: karate, gymnastics, tennis, swimming, football, basketball, soccer, wrestling, and his favorite, skateboarding. Gramma was proud.

In first grade, Jovanni showed signs of multiple learning disabilities, which didn't surprise me. I could help, and I did. The details of which could fill another book.

The key to Jovanni's academic survival was being in an I.E.P, Individual Education Program, with the public school system, having the support of many committed teachers, and an advocate: Gramma. At 19, he received a hard-earned high school diploma.

Happily, Jovanni was a good-looking kid with a flair for style, a ready smile, and loyal friends.

Chapter 29: Fitness Career

When it sunk in that I would most likely be teaching fitness for a long time, I got serious.

Teaching active seniors, from age 50 to the end of life, is radically different from teaching rehab patients in a hospital. Rather than a single room for classes and a small gym with weights, I would now be teaching at Sun City Anthem in Henderson, Nevada, one of the finest, best-equipped, and professionally staffed facilities in the country.

Quickly, I studied for and received a certification from The American Senior Fitness Association. Senior fitness is different from under 50 fitness in many ways. I traveled to California to be certified in Yoga Fit: Yoga for the Fitness Industry, Levels I, II, and III. I got CPR and insurance coverage. I invested in stylish fitness clothes, got my hair trimmed and nails polished, and washed my car.

It took a few years for my classes to develop and grow, which was a good thing. There was so much to learn and understand that it felt like I was apprenticing for the "real thing," just around the corner. I had to upgrade my knowledge base and develop new skills, strength, and stamina to take on students who were younger and in better shape than I was. I was now 70.

Contrary to the prevalent mindset of the day, we were more than just a bunch of "old folks" barely moving. We were on the cusp of a new trend: Senior Fitness, fitness for life-long health, exercising with friends and neighbors, social bonding. We were a kaleidoscopic crowd from diverse backgrounds. We hailed from a time in history going back many years. Many of us had lived through The Great Depression, World War II, the exuberant '50s, turbulent '60s, pivotal '70s, rockin' '80s, confusing '90s, and we survived. We'd had careers, marriages, and the responsibilities of raising children during those times. We shared stories of our struggles and successes. We became a movement.

Not that we shared life's intimate details; we'd been taught to respect privacy. Nor did we chat while exercising. However, there was ample social time to meet and befriend like-minded folks.

Human lifespan had bolted 20 years beyond our generation's expectation. While that was great news, we had not anticipated needing to take care of ourselves for that long. We certainly weren't prepared to care of our failing spouses, parents, and often our children for another 20 years. Mostly women and a few men would now spend their retirement years as caregivers.

That reality gave impetus and importance to the Senior Fitness Movement. We had to be in better shape than we had ever anticipated.

Anthem offered current fitness programs as well as traditional classes and workout routines. Over the next 13 years, I taught a variety of formats, such as Workout Sitting Down, Silver and Fit, Trim and Tone (aerobics and strength), Bellies and Buns (core), '80s Retro Floor Work (deep core), Beaming (balance), Gliding (inner thigh work), Body Ball (strength and stretch), Cognitive Fitness Facilitator (brain function and memory), basic Yoga Fit, Power Yoga for Athletes, and Laughter Yoga (euphoric laughing).

To expand my student base, I cut back to half-time at Anthem and began teaching additional classes at Sun City MacDonald Ranch, Humana Guidance Center, and Merrill Gardens Assisted Living in 2007. In 2013, I created and taught Gentle Yoga for Students with Multiple Sclerosis under a grant from the Multiple Sclerosis Foundation.

I enjoyed consistent student participation, not only because I was a contemporary in excellent health, but also because I had a marvelous collection of fitness music by genre. One day, we would work out to favorite music of the '50s, and another day to a Broadway Musical, another to '80s rock. Nothing like music to get folks moving.

Those years of bopping around with so many folks my age were priceless.

I learned through experience that regular exercise brings energy, strength, flexibility, better balance, sharper minds, and a lovely sense of long-term well-being to all who embrace it. No pills, lotions, potions, food, diet, can deliver the same effect. The more classes and variety of classes I taught, the better I felt.

Up to a limit, of course. My limit was teaching three or four classes a day compacted into the morning hours. In my late 70s, it became harder to keep up that pace. At 80, I cut back due to decreasing stamina and arthritis in my feet. By 82, I was physically spent. I retired at 83.

I had to accept that bodies do eventually break down, even when you're healthy. I'd been in denial about that for a long time. Little suspicions, but nothing significant until age 80, when it became apparent: I was shorter, weaker, had a sloppy belly, sliding boobs, deeper wrinkles, turkey neck, whiskers on my chin, arthritic feet, dentures, cataracts, hearing loss, and an escalation in my short-term memory malfunction. Darn!

Most everyone seems to have a personal moment in time when it starts. Different scenarios. Different reactions.

Students gathered to give me a bodacious retirement party. Fun, music, food, presents, lots of hugs, kisses, best wishes, and a GoFundMe retirement account that enabled me to move and settle in a small town in Florida, be near Beth, my oldest child, and create the next chapter of my life—which I am doing.

So many of my students had benefitted from their years of exercise that I had begun to sense my mission in life was to inspire folks who were growing older to create the best possible lives for themselves by sharing my knowledge and experience when appropriate. My fitness career, however, had been that of teaching only exercise classes. My job descriptions bound me to stay focused on exercise, not to give advice on other matters, or try to sell products or divert student interest in any way.

But I knew that fitness embraces more than exercise. Foods and nutrition matter and I hadn't been sleeping on that fact. I'd been reading books and following food and nutrition activity on the internet. I was always looking for a way to blend both without compromising my income.

Five years earlier, such an opportunity had surreptitiously presented itself.

Chapter 30: Becoming a Writer

In 2009, I decided to try internet marketing to promote the fitness DVDs I had filmed with and for my students at Anthem.

A journalist friend referred me to an online marketing coach to guide me. She referred me to the web and graphic designer, Design by Shoi, to develop the necessary tools for online marketing: branding, a website, a newsletter, and special reports. I loved Shoi's artistic style and professionalism.

Caroline's Fitness DVDs for Seniors
(Now sold out)

I contacted everyone I knew to share my new internet business, and they were nice, but basically, nothing happened.

My online coach suggested that perhaps my credentials were not "fresh" enough to attract customers or a following. She recommended that I update my credentials to establish credibility. Or write and publish a book. I wasn't about to go back to school, nor did I have a clue about writing a book. It looked like the end of my dream.

Then I heard about Write a Book in a Weekend Workshop. Get a book written that could be used as a "big business card" to promote me and my product. It didn't have to be a great book since "just being a published author is enough for marketing purposes."

I signed up and received a couple hundred pages of information including templates online. The next week, on a Thursday evening, I met with other hopefuls sharing this online training. The workshop leader said, "Pack in some ready-to-eat food and get rid of your family for the weekend. Pick a topic you know something about and just start writing and never stop. No fixes, no edits, just write." I did. I wrote all weekend steadily, and as I wrote, the words and ideas began to take form. Like magic, the ideas became a table of contents.

We students met on conference calls again on Saturday morning and evening, and on Sunday night to close the workshop. After all that writing, sore fingers and watering eyes, I had only 38 pages. Not enough for a book. But we slow pokes were gifted two more weeks to finish. So I kept writing, mentioning other lifestyle behaviors that enhanced a healthy life and telling stories from my experience that supported the main ideas, incorporating them until I had enough pages for a thin book. With large print.

It wasn't a finished product, nor did it have a title. The workshop leader said she'd take a look down the road if I ever got it done.

With help from students, my to-be book got a title: *The Curious Upside of Growing Older and the 7 Keys that Active Seniors Embrace for the Best Life.* Another student, a retired English professor, edited it. After editing and polishing it, the workshop leader approved it.

The book was now ready for formatting. The company, Done for You Publishing, got it ready; Shoi created the cover. I submitted it to Lightning Source who published it in April 2011.

I gave copies to my family, friends, and students and asked them to write reviews. By June, it was on Amazon with five 5-Star reader reviews. From my students.

I sold more books than DVDs. But I didn't care. At this point, I was busily writing about everything fitness without getting in trouble at work.

In January 2011, I followed up by introducing *FitBits Newsletter: News You Can Use.*

FITBITS NEWSLETTER

The first *FitBits* was published on January 28, 2011. *FitBits Newsletter* is published by Constant Contact; it has earned their All-Star Award every year since then, based mainly on reader loyalty.

FitBits opens up like this: "Thank you for opening my newsletter today. *FitBits* does its best to bring you outside-the-box news bytes that will keep you involved in the all-important fields of mind and body fitness, and on occasion, may entertain you."

FitBits is free, timely, and always upbeat. Skim time is under two minutes with 'Click Here' links to read the full articles. The main article is usually about food and/or nutrition. This allows me to disseminate factual and useful information while building a following of like-minded people.

There was lots of news to share. I was hardly the only person dismayed by the bullish hand of the food industry. New books were out, secrets exposed. Soon, books were offering insight, history, and solutions.

ᘓ Wayward Trends ᘓ

The cultural move away from traditional thinking about food and nutrition kept gaining ground. But family gardens and home cooking weren't making money for anyone. I was just waking up to the obvious, that industrial food had the financial strength and the tools to push their agenda onto an unsuspecting, uneducated populace via television, the internet, and celebrity endorsements. And to the fact that this was not new news.

With the FDA's permission to create unnatural food products, hundreds of thousands have come to market. Cultural jargon has dubbed them fake foods, Frankenfood, faux food, ersatz food, virtual food, non-food food, designer food, science-based food, engineered food, nutrient-free food, and plastic food.

They are "food" only in the loosest sense of the word. Some may have once been real food, but have quietly been reformulated over time. These products are not created by nature. Legally, they are not subject to nutritional transparency. Only limited ingredient labeling is required. Nonetheless, they are considered to be real food by most people.

Another trend is the over-simplification of food words and use of ambiguous terms. These have become cultural habits that make meaningful conversations about the issues or problems difficult to have.

For instance: salt. There is table salt (pure sodium chloride, which is a by-product of the manufacture of explosives, chlorine gas, baking soda, fertilizers, and plastic.). And there is unrefined salt (from ancient sea beds and which contains 80 or more minerals essential for good health). These two salts are not the same.

'Beef' became 'red meat.' 'Fat' became 'saturated fat' though oils are fat in liquid form. 'Protein' is considered to be a single thing. However, there are infinite proteins in nature with known functions in our bodies and man-made proteins about which we know little.

A single food word may have many variations. Carrots, for example. There are different species grown in different soils at different times of the year, harvested differently, freshly picked or processed. And they aren't all the same. They differ in nutritional value. Another example: 'red meat' can be from healthy animals or tortured animals. The quality of the flesh is a reflection of the treatment of the animal. Foods can be prepared with a heavy hand or a gentle hand. Their nutritional value will differ.

In most cases, the reported content of nutrients in the foods we eat is based on foods at their peak before shipping, storage, before processing. Just numbers from the *USDA Food Composition Data Bases*.

Adding to our confusion, there are two distinct approaches to understanding health itself: holistic and reductionist. Holistic deals with the whole bodily system operating as one with synergism. Reductionists hold that a complex system can be better understood in terms of its simpler components. 'Dinner' is holistic. Separately analyzing each of the macro and micronutrients, vitamins and minerals, nutraceuticals, antioxidants, etc. in 'dinner' is reductionist.

∽ Oppressive Trends ∽

- Large-scale efforts to confuse customers
- Deceptive organizations
  See the six appendices in "Appetite for Profit"[3]
- Using the media to manipulate and terrify customers
- Drug-to-consumer advertising – Way up
- Food-to-consumer advertising – Unregulated
- Popularizing diets based on unfounded or questionable information
  See link "600 Diets" in Appendix 4
- Creating medical-sounding names for natural conditions like Female Sexual Dysfunction (lack of desire for sex), Social Anxiety Disorder

---

Appetite for Profit: How the Food Industry Undermines Our Health and How to Fight Back - Michelle Simon, 2006, Basic Books.

(shyness), and Osteopenia (aging, yet healthy bones). And turning "risks" into medical conditions. Shaping public perceptions.
See "Selling Sickness"[4]

- Hiding unhealthy food ingredients
  See "Hidden Sources of Sugar" in Appendix 4
  See "Hidden Sources of MSG" in Appendix 4
- Food contamination
- Adulterated food products
- Increasing numbers of laws to harass and close down small farmers and artisans
- Defying actual science, as with genetically modified organisms (GMOs)
- Legitimizing pseudo-science with massive media exposure

✑ Forward-Looking Trends ✑

- The robust growth and expansion of grassroots food movements from farm to table
- Increased defense of science and real research (the fight is on)
- An increase of young people with knowledge and optimism
- Exposure of animal cruelty, overuse of farmland, and ecological ignorance
- A surge of consumer demand for healthier food and honesty in advertising
- Healthy lifestyle trends that include physical fitness, enough sleep, and socialization

All this is confusing. What a giant mess our food and nutrition culture had gotten us into. I found plenty of stories for *FitBits*.

✑ Personal Life ✑

Early on, my life in Vegas had been filled with raising Jovanni and working. As he matured and found his own entertainment, I had a chance to make some adult friends and get out on occasion. I would hike up at Red Rock, occasionally went dancing, saw a few shows down on the Strip. It had been a restrictive existence. I did have a guy friend for most of those years. I'd never had a guy friend before; it was enlightening, comforting.

But fourteen years of teaching fitness in Vegas, a tired body, Jovanni graduating high school, and the guardianship automatically terminating

---

[4] *Selling Sickness: How the World's Biggest Pharmaceutical Companies Are Turning Us All Into Patients* - Ray Moynihan & Alan Cassels, 2005, Nation Books.

made this the perfect time to move on. Jovanni took my leaving hard, but staying longer wouldn't have made it any easier for him, or me.

I picked out only the things I really wanted to move across country: my bed, books, files, computer, pictures, linens and some kitchen things, and gave the rest away. I boxed them up, put them in a U-Haul pod and shipped them to storage in Gainesville, Florida. I put my clothes in my car and sent it to Beth on an auto transporter.

I hugged my long-time massage therapist, my manicurist, and my hair stylist, all of whom had dutifully listened to the ongoing litany of my trials and tribulations over the years. I hugged a few close friends, gathered up our cat, Geno, put him in a carrier, and off we flew to my next adventure. It was October 2015; I was 83.

Chapter 31: Retired

That's a funny word. 'Retired.' Like I'm tired again. Like putting a new tire on where a worn out one used to be. The word fits. I spent most of my first month in Florida sleeping. Geno paced and yowled.

There were many days of driving around looking for a place to live somewhere near Beth, near where I'd had the sign company. Quite a few of my signs are still standing after all of the years. A homecoming of sorts.

Luck was with me. A friend of Beth's heard of an apartment coming available on December 1st in an old (circa 1883) hotel in a small town just south of Beth's place. The hotel was charming; the apartment was beyond perfect: upstairs, roomy with windows on four sides. It came partially furnished with antiques, overlooked the town's library on the front side, and had a big, gorgeous, green yard with trees on the back side. Behind that were train tracks with trains running several times a day, reminding me of my life in Flagstaff when I was a kid. Thrilled, I moved in.

I set about meeting people. The library was a likely place, always lots going on. I joined the book club. In March, I gave a talk at the library on *The Curious Upside of Growing Older*, and another one in October about Neurobics (mind games). Also, I joined the local gym, dilapidated, but the owner let me use the one room to teach. I volunteered to teach a seated exercise class to the Super Seniors Group (six people on a good day) and offered yoga in April, which soon grew. Beth and Barb gave me an adult tricycle for Christmas, so I get a good ride down a forest trail four or five times a week.

Not having a steady job, I've downsized my expectations and expenses. There are abundant gardens all about, so finding fresh in-season veggies is easy. Backyard chickens provide eggs for all. Strawberry and blueberry fields overflow during their season. Citrus season spans several months. The folks at the Food Bank call me "the soup lady," saving me bones and meat for broth. I drive into Gainesville once a week for a gallon of raw milk, butter, and cheese. Folks take care of one another here, sharing casserole dishes and friendship.

It's like stepping back in time, reliving my childhood in The Depression—so comforting.

Mostly, my life here has been quiet, peaceful. I read and catch up with the world via the internet, keep up with *FitBits*. I began writing this book; I'd been thinking about it for a long time. I had intended it to be a documentary of sorts, following foods and nutrition since The Depression, telling my story to show the education and experience it takes to be knowledgeable, to be trustworthy.

I enlisted several willing *FitBits* readers to assist me by editing my drafts for content and clarity. After a couple chapters, they let me know, "It's boring," that only details of living in those times were engaging. So I expanded the text to include some detail of life in those days. My readers liked the story better, but grumbled, "No spice?"

"What?" I replied, "You want me to tell about my private, personal life? Secrets I have been hiding forever?"

"Yes."

Wow. That would be a big scary stretch for me. I had to ruminate on that one for a while.

In February 2017, my daughter Beth and friends took buses to DC to join the Woman's March, women standing up for women's issues, for equality, and for respect. I followed every minute on TV. Powerful. I went to the Gainesville Woman's meeting a few days later. The large room was packed, overflowing into the parking lot with passionate women and supportive men with an agenda to cause change.

I heard women's stories, felt their anguish and anger. Yes, I had my own personal experience and snippets about the women in my family generations back, but that was it. I had no knowledge of anyone else; we all kept secrets, knew little of women's history.

So I read *Who Cooked the Last Supper: The Women's History of the World.* That opened up a Pandora's Box of information—from the beginning, when women were worshiped because they could handle all the home and family needs, could bleed at will and create babies inside of themselves. Goddesses ruled. The whole belief system changed as men learned that their sperm was necessary for procreation. Men took power. Women were relegated to slavery status and kept there using despotic tactics; many are still in place today, held there by the habits of cultural custom and religious dogma.

I realized that the secrets I had so carefully guarded all my life were in response to the fear of being deemed "unacceptable" because I had been "soiled" (raped), am an alcoholic (lacked self-respect), couldn't read (stupid), had yearnings (a slut), unwanted pregnancy (promiscuous), abortion (baby killer), was over-educated (entitled), too smart (false pride), couldn't make a marriage work (didn't try hard enough).

To be "found out" would/could result in swift and unrelenting degradation and punishment. For such sins, women were disowned by their families, expelled from their church, lost their children, lost their livelihood, and other horrors.

Clearly, my secrets were to hide my "defects."

Which are defects only in a patriarchal society.

So I took my pride in hand, braced myself, and decided to share my secrets in this book—especially the ways patriarchy had been my master, how I had willingly submitted, and why.

As I was re-editing the draft of my book, I had an odd feeling, a physical sensation, like I'd just lost weight. Or something. It left me feeling light, high.

And then, something else happened. My memories became vivid, especially during wakeful sleep. There was detail, emotion. Day and night for about two weeks. I wasn't trying to remember; they just came. Some that I had written about came again, enhanced with detail.

We had just returned to Maryland. I would be working in the chem lab with an assistant, "Old John." When I greeted him that first morning, he turned on me with fire in his eyes. "Never in my life did I think they'd make me kowtow to a woman. Never!" He fumed. "You women are just trying to steal a man's livelihood. That's all. You're sick. Mad because you wish you were a man." Long silence; I didn't move. Then, in a resigned tone, "I won't put up with it, that's what. I'll quit. That's what."

"But John, you're just about to retire. Couldn't we get along till then?"

"No. I have dignity." Old John retired early.

 భ

Jovanni was saying goodnight to a girl. My clock said 5 a.m. I got up and followed him back to his room. "Jovanni, did that girl spend the night here?"

"Yup."

"Did you—"

"Yup."

"Do you know, uh, . . . "

"Yes, Gramma," he said opening the drawer of his bedside table. There were condoms inside. He closed the drawer. "Is there anything else you would like to know?"

"Um, . . . no, I guess not."

With a smile in his voice, he said, "Gramma, if there is ever anything you want to know, don't be shy, just ask, OK?"

"I'm really out of touch," I said to myself.

༭

I was with David. We were in Greenwich Village. In 1960 or 61.

We were sitting at a small round table in a coffee shop. David was sitting up straight. He always sat up straight; not stiff, just straight. Alert and attentive. And handsome: blue oxford cloth shirt, bold stripe on his tie. In his tweed blazer with leather patches on the elbows.

It was a small, warm coffee shop smelling of people, tobacco. A raised platform to one side. A nut-brown man was reading his poem in a soft, mesmerizing, melancholy voice. Every so often, he would pause and look around at his listeners; we were returning his gaze, deep into his message.

David turned and smiled at me. A warm smile; his eyes sparkled. I smiled back, happy.

I awoke. It was 3:30 a.m. This was not a dream. It was a memory. Vivid. Real. I remember the coffee shop.

I fell back asleep.

David and I were standing in a crowd at the Village Gate on Bleeker Street listening to Dave Brubeck and his new Quartet. The mood was high-spirited, raucous at times. David was in heaven; I was tired. There was no place to sit down.

I woke up unusually late that morning. I must have had a good time in my memory last night.

I had dozens of such random enhanced-memories, some relevant to my secrets, some not.

I try to explain this to myself. The original event happened, of course. If that event was frightful, painful, drew red flags, I kept it as a secret, locked it in, so to speak. When I began to share my secrets in this book, they didn't seem so bad.

If there is any logic to this, it must be that letting go of long-held secrets triggers a healing release.

For example:

Then, John was a fool, but now, I understand he'd been brought up that way. Then, I was upset that Jovanni broke our house rules; now, I see that he was straight up about it and showed respect for the girl. I'm reminded that I loved David early in our marriage and blamed my secret "defects" for its demise.

I accept that such defects were legitimate then, but can no longer harm me. Times have changed. Attitudes have changed. I have changed. My memories are real only in the history of that moment in time. The memories are still with me, but the fear dissolved when I put them in perspective. Now I can actually enjoy memories of times past and embrace the lessons learned.

All this remembering has me thinking, re-evaluating my life. My whole history; who was me, is no more. I've been catching insights, deeper meaning, lessons, and gratitude for the life I have lived.

INSIGHTS

This patriarchal culture has not ruined my life—not at all.

My resolve is strong. The rape, the abuse, the verbal and emotional degradation, the humiliating moments, the laws by men for men to lord over women, the fear that I might not be able to feed my kids: these were merely the challenges that tested me. Our culture taught me to play dumb, hide, and slither along in the shadows.

But no more! Now I'm motivated to "un-hide," to challenge patriarchy, experts, popular science, and Big Food. No one can fire me now; I'm retired!

∽ FOODS AND NUTRITION ∽
Then and Now

In 1932, mile-high Flagstaff, Arizona, had about 3,300 residents, a mixed bag of Caucasians, Mexicans, and Hopi Indians. Astronomers at Lowell Observatory north of Flagstaff had just confirmed the discovery of Planet X, later named Pluto.

Socially, each ethnic group stuck together. But we all ate what there was to eat: beef and hog; quail and deer; eggs, milk, butter, and cheese; vegetables in season; crab apples; home-canned tomatoes and string beans; oatmeal and farina; homemade bread and desserts. Dinner was a family affair.

We believed that food was provided by Mother Nature, energized by Father Sun, and nurtured by humans, stewards of the planet. We were grateful.

People were rarely sick except for kids getting measles, mumps, and chicken pox. My school friend, Emily, and her mom were the only fat people in town. Heredity, they said.

I ate my first fast food at MacDonald's when it opened in DC in 1956. The food was prepared in-house fresh each day; hamburger was from local cows, French fries were sliced from raw potatoes and double-fried in "all-purpose cooking fat," a mixture of tallow, lard and "plastic fat" like Crisco. Delicious.

In the early '60s, I started buying processed foods like breakfast cereal for my young girls because it was advertised on kids' TV programs. But I still home-cooked natural, traditional meals even after fast food began to show up all over.

As I write this in 2017, eating habits have switched. Eating regular dinners at home has declined; many meals and snack items are eaten outside the home. Industrial foods are common wherever people eat.

As a result, most people no longer eat just the products of nature. They consume nutrients and chemicals, the products of food science and industry.

Here's the problem: <u>The body cannot make the food it needs from processed nutrients and chemicals. Such consumers are always hungry, never satisfied.</u>

In 2015, *Science News* reported that highly processed foods make up more than 60 percent of the calories in the food we buy. The Boston Medical Center tells us that "approximately 45 million Americans diet each year and spend $33 billion on weight-loss products in their pursuit of a trimmer, fitter body." They also found that 20 percent of all meals are eaten in the car.

In May 2016, the Centers for Disease Control and Prevention reported that the 70.7 percent of adults age 20 and over were overweight, including obesity.

ᖰ WHAT HAPPENED? ᖰ
Here's a Brief Timeline

Over a century ago, the industrial revolution made equipment and production plants that streamlined food production. Trains and trucks began transporting food.

The development of farming equipment spurred increased production. To keep pace, chemical fertilizers were used to speed up plant growth, as traditional agricultural practices were too slow. Profits of industrial agriculture went up; small and family farms decreased.

The soil of commercial farms became imbalanced, depleted of essential plant nutrients. The weakened plants attracted insects; pesticides like DDT were born. Over time, the detrimental effects began to affect people, causing illness.

Food packaging and supermarkets sprung up.

WWII spearheaded the need for transportable foods with longer shelf-life. The food industry responded with processed foods and non-food foods. Research found chemicals and food additives that made these foods possible. Scientists questioned their safety.

After the war, many women continued working, welcoming time-saving foods, like boxed and frozen foods, to keep up with family needs. We all assumed these were healthy foods.

TV came into our homes. With advertising. Business boomed. But general health began to decrease. Heart disease increased.

In 1961, the American Heart Association launched the low-fat diet onto the public, believing it would decrease heart disease. It eliminates saturated fats (necessary for good health) and promotes unhealthy oils. Unfortunately, the diet has not reduced heart disease. Obesity is one of the unintended side effects.

In 1963, the FDA bowed to the food industry by changing the legal definition of food. Traditionally, food is defined as a "nutritious substance that people or animals eat or drink, or that plants absorb, to maintain life and growth." The legal definition now is "(1) articles used for food or drink for man or other animals, (2) chewing gum, and (3) articles used for components of any such article."

With the doors open and all restraints removed, the food industry launched into the market a tsunami of manufactured "foods," sold with impunity. These "food products" do not meet the human need for nutrition. People began to malfunction.

In the mid '70s, organic farmers adopted the first standards for organic produce and certification of organic farms began.

In the mid '90s the "Information Age" was born. With advertising.

Food supplements showed up and were exempted from the safeguards required of food and pharmaceuticals.

Big Pharma got into the act, selling cholesterol-lowering drugs, even after scientists had demonstrated that there was no relationship between blood cholesterol and heart health.

Diets became more popular. Diets eliminating or diminishing an essential food or food groups and diets recommending imbalanced nutrition have failed to bring about better health long-term. (See

Appendix 2, The ABCs of Nutrition and Appendix 3, Snake-Oil Salesmen.)

Claiming prevention, Big Pharma started selling pharmaceuticals to healthy people. (That's not the way the body works.)

Big Pharma and Big Food began creating many of today's "diseases" and "conditions," which are actually standard bodily functions to be "cured or managed" with their products.

The Information Age has morphed into the age of misinformation—bolstered by excessive advertising.

* * *

Is it surprising that so many people faithfully follow the cultural advice but don't get the promised results? Feel lousy? Cry, struggle, may have to work more hours to pay for the treatments and meds? Do they know that evil industries trick and lie to them? Industries that need to sell more and more to satisfy their investors?

ᕳ WE CAN TURN THIS AROUND ᕲ

It's already happening. Every day, people make the switch back to natural foods and medicines. You can, too.

First, stop supporting the industrial foods industry; don't buy their products. Eat fresh local natural pesticide-free foods in season. And organic when possible. These foods provide nutrients and energy.

Industrial/factory foods are awash with modified ingredients, food particles, pesticides, mysterious compounds, and chemicals that our bodies do not recognize. Our bodies cannot metabolize them.

Avoid trendy diets, extreme diets, diets that vilify essential foods or food groups. A person's best diet is based his or her family history, general health, and lifestyle and then modified to their specific needs and desires. Modification is ongoing as life is in constant change, just as our bodies and their needs are.

The only "diet" I know that is effective long-term is a traditional diet based on natural foods. Why? We need the sun's energy that comes to us via nature's food chain. Our bodies know how to use natural food. Our bodies have synergistic abilities far beyond our understanding.

I don't try to tell anyone what to eat because I don't know. Neither does anyone else. There are too many possibilities. There are roughly 7.5 billion people on the planet (2017). There are over 600 diets in the US.

(Appendix 4) What are the chances of someone else knowing the right foods for you?

Every possibility is just somebody's "idea."

Realize that one's health depends on many factors besides diet. Eating only natural food is essential, but not enough. We must consider lifestyle, genetics, age, health, and so on.

Take a look at "Caroline's Recipe for Wellness" (Appendix 6). It offers an easy way to get started. My first book, *The Curious Upside of Growing Older: And the 7 Keys that Active Seniors Embrace for the Best Life* stresses the vital importance of living a balanced life.

Please, don't stress over what to eat. <u>Be calm</u>. You don't need to worry about all that sketchy chatter that bombards us daily. Just eat small, simple meals of natural foods, 10-inch plates, no seconds, no dessert. Get restful sleep, exercise regularly, get outside and play in the sunshine; share time with friends. Try it. You might like it.

There is an appendix at the end of this book where you will find trustworthy information to support you in: 1) understanding the essentials of food and nutrition, and (2) making good food choices. No fluff. No crap.

- Appendix 1 - Food Words – Clarifying Definitions

- Appendix 2 - The ABCs of Nutrition – Size, Metabolism, and Balance

- Appendix 3 – Snake-Oil Salesmen – Experts, Orchestrating Consumption, Slick and Slippery Words and Phrases, and Popular Science

- Appendix 4 - Links to Hidden Sources of Sugar, Hidden Sources of MSG, and Over 600 Diets

- Appendix 5 - What Do I Eat?

- Appendix 6 - Recipe for Wellness

- Appendix 7 - Reliable Resources – Books, Articles, and Organizations

- Appendix 8 - Documentation of My Research

∽ ON BEING A WOMAN ∽

My ignorance was predetermined and stifled my path.

Not that I chose ignorance. It was the culture I was born into. It had been here for thousands of years. Men could only be in charge of the world if women were submissive. The most effective tactic to maintain the status quo was to keep women ignorant. So women were held housebound, relegated to household tasks, raising the children, and servicing the men.

I wasn't aware of this. How could I have known? Women taught their daughters survival skills, woman's work, generation after generation. Even if women had been allowed an education, the books were written by men. History was about men. Religion was crafted by men for men. God was a man.

In charge, men made the rules, policies, and laws that block women's desire to learn, to advance. Quite effective is the pervasive degradation of all things woman, true or not. From Aristotle to today, men innately consider women to be weaker, of low intelligence, overly emotional, disgusting (menstruation), etc. Women who have stepped out of the mold have been largely ignored or severely chastised.

Women in my family had stepped out of the mold. Great Gramma crossed over the Oregon Trail when she was 12, set up a day-school and taught while raising nine children. Dad's mother and Aunt Sarah both graduated from Stanford in the 1890s, having careers. Mom's mom leaving Germany alone at age 17, to "seek her fortune" in America. Mom earned her master's degree in Histology with a dream that never materialized. They encouraged me to step out and be independent. ("You never know when you might have to support yourself.")

In college, their advice began to register. I was one of the few females taking basic science classes. I went into science to show my Dad that I wasn't dumb, that I could be somebody. I sensed that he was proud of me, though it would have been unfitting for him to let on.

During the 10 years of my foods and nutrition research career, I noticed that most professional women were teachers, nurses, or office staff, more mainstream than being a scientist.

All was well until I got pregnant. That's when my house of cards began tumbling down.

I woke up, realized I'd been lucky, tolerated by society. I'd walked the tightrope, earning our living as I supported my contemptuous husband, raised our children, and managed our home. When I crumbled, breaking loose was hard with those men-made laws designed to keep me in my place. Wouldn't let me have a personal bank account or file for divorce or make other choices for my health and well-being of my children. I felt the doors close around me.

It seemed that I had failed somehow, disappointed the women who believed in me, been too arrogant to discern reality. But there was no time to lick my wounds. I had children to feed.

I found a way.

Now, many years later, I understand that my situation wasn't just my ignorance or my fault. It is the ignorance of a paternalistic society that makes the rules. How irrational is it that women are charged with the care of themselves, of their husbands and children, but are shackled from doing so by archaic practices? Our culture of men depends on women for their survival, then they bite the hands that feed them.

* * *

Now I see that my struggles forced me to follow a different path, and in so doing, to experience an adventurous life.

I bounced around, falling into a variety of unique, non-academic jobs, where I got to know all kinds of people. I liked them, not as stuffy as in academia. These jobs enabled me to live in geographical areas where people think differently: The Midwest, Out West, Deep South, New England, Mid-Atlantic, DC, Maryland, and Florida. Tiny towns, college towns, large cities. Always, people are different in their talk, dress, customs, and attitude.

I got the chance to participate in social movements: Back to the Land connecting with the earth; New Age with visions, many of which are now a reality; the resurgence of organic and traditional foods honoring our ancestors.

I had a second chance to share life with a partner, this time with a man who loved me unconditionally.

I raised three generations of children, mostly by myself, learning about and guiding their hopes and dreams, engaging in their fluctuating interests, living in homes that vibrated with their music.

And, I wound up loving an unexpected 20-year career in fitness, serving health-minded adults from many walks of life, keeping myself healthy at the same time.

Probably more fun than having been a research nutritionist for 50 years.

⌇ SECRETS ⌇

Like so many folks, I've held carefully guarded secrets all my life.

Letting them go, on paper, to the entire world so that I could be rightly hated, chastised, and banished would have happened 20, 30, or 40 years ago. But now, telling all was merely a heart-thumping decision. And a huge relief. I feel clean. Now I can look at these events with fresh eyes.

Every woman has a secret or two or more. And men, as well. Letting go works wonders, even if you only put it in writing or tell just one person. Try it. You'll feel ever so much better.

⌇ PREGNANCY ⌇

After my divorce, I was trying to be social, challenging for an introvert. The pill was new and "virtually 100% effective." I went for it and got pregnant anyhow like many others at that time. I learned what "virtually" means. Not much. The to-be father was unfazed; "Women get pregnant to get quality husbands."

I was unmarried and really in a pickle. I sought an abortion, illegal in Florida. I took a chance; the consequences were horrendous.

I'd had trouble finding and keeping a job after my divorce. I was a woman who had the audacity to file for divorce, not my right. How dare I? And, encumbered with children, I was unreliable as an employee because I would always put the children first. And now, with an illegal abortion on my rap sheet, things were even worse. I was a loose person, disgusting, dirty, immoral, a slut.

Many women face these dilemmas. There is a solution. It's a simple concept. It takes sperm to impregnate a woman. The unborn child has two parents: a father and a mother. The problem is that in this patriarchal society, the father can avoid responsibility in a myriad of ways and walk away. Men often choose this option. Unto this day, unless you are incredibly fortunate, pregnancy comes back to the woman to handle.

The man who impregnates the woman - you know, the one who didn't wear a condom because he didn't have time, or it would interfere with his pleasure - is the father of the resulting child. Period. We have DNA now.

Here's a solution: We must hold in the heart of our society the undeniable fact that the impregnating man *is* the father of the child, that he is equally responsible for the child's life until emancipation. Should the father refuse, he must be "fixed": have his tubes tied and forced, whatever that takes, to pay half of the expenses of raising a child, which is hefty. Not to mention the cost of mom's time and energy, attention, and health.

Surely our society can be schooled to understand that it is irrational to demand that a woman be responsible for raising a child she didn't ask for. I've experienced this abuse firsthand, and I have no stomach for men who dodge responsibility by blaming the woman.

When laws are passed, and enforced, requiring men to bear equal responsibility, I'll bet prevention will get popular real fast.

This solution can start in preschool with stories: "this is a mommy" and "this is a daddy." Each year, add a bit more information. In middle school, a young man should learn the whole thing, from STDs to how to please a woman. I'm serious.

My abortion was not a murderous act, but a necessary choice, given my options at the time. Words cannot describe the anguish of being forced to make such a choice.

I am pro-birth, pro-childhood, pro-teenhood, pro-emancipation, pro-20s, pro-30s, pro-40s, pro-50s all the way to the end, and then I am pro-death. But I am not for forced, solitary, unsupported, unwanted pregnancy.

❧ AM I A MAN-HATER? ❧
Not at All

Remember, my telling you that I walked away from all habits I thought might weaken my resolve to maintain sobriety, to be in control of my life? I said "no sex." That was 36 years ago; I am still celibate. My choice for celibacy wasn't because I hated men.

Most men are good people, allies in wanting a good life for all. I would have preferred a loving partnership with a man, but I was not willing to retake the chance of misjudging, winding up with abuse until the end of my life. In time, I have grown to relish the time and freedom of celibacy.

Raising Jovanni gave me a vision of hope for the future. He and his friends were born in the mid '90s. The Information Age was born at the same time. It is no longer easy for society to hide knowledge. These kids are sharp and curious. They support one another. They show me more respect than older men do.

My angst is with violent men and rapists, about 33 percent of the male population.[5]

---

[5] *WHO: Violence Against Women Is An 'Epidemic' Global Health Problem: 2013*

∾ RAPE ∾

I hold rape as a heinous crime that many men joke about. It's not funny. Some rapists get a slap on the hand from the judge, a supportive snicker from the guys, and a congratulatory pat on his back from Dad for scoring his "10 minutes of action."

NO!

Rape is wicked, evil, depraved abuse. It is not about sex. It is about conquest, power, and control. It began 5,000 to 7,000 years ago when waves of marauders swept down upon peaceful, productive cultures, taking their lands, killing the men, and impregnating the women, and then ruling with force and fear. This was the cradle of patriarchy, supported over time by man-made religion and by destroying women's history. Read *The Chalice and the Blade.* (See Appendix 7.)

Addressing the issue of rape will be tough as rape is trivialized by patriarchy. No, we cannot "treat" a rapist with counseling, rehab, or jail. Rape devastates for a lifetime. Equivalent punishment is in order. Those committing serious sex offenses should undergo surgical castration. Additional punishment must be imposed if the victims are children. For lesser sex offenses, chemical castration may suffice. Then, the criminal is to be assigned jobs that serve society, such as farming. We'll figure things out.

Understandably, righteous folks will cringe at this. However, such treatment is kinder than the violent acts inflicted on girls and women for thousands of years for far lesser "crimes." Read *Who Cooked the Last Supper: The Women's History of the World.* (See Appendix 7.)

Heads-up, ladies. Sexism thrives. Female genital mutilation is being practiced worldwide. In America, 513,000 girls/women were at risk in 2012. Christianity, Judaism, and Muslimism are complicit with genital mutilation and disfigurement. Sex trafficking is huge. Brute-force abuse is rampant and acceptable.

In many cases, domestic abuse and child abuse laws now protect women and children. Mostly, there is judicial hesitancy to interfere in domestic matters. In a man's primal mind, it's his right as a husband and father to "control" his wife and children as he sees fit.

Patriarchy will continue until we stop it. Not an easy task. It has been entrenched for centuries. By now, it's probably in man's DNA. But, it must be dealt with for the survival of humankind.

Wars aren't won by whining and complaining. Exposure and public shaming are good. *But not good enough.* Battles are won by taking on the opponent at his own game. I'm not suggesting guns, bombs, or chemical warfare, but massive legal and social intervention. Women have gained a toe-hold in the politics and laws of this and many other countries. Their efforts are escalating. We must double-down and join them, support them. We can do it. There are millions of us.

We need laws that not only punish, but that are severe enough to deter harassment, abuse, cruelty, and rape.

Women and supportive men must fight today with the passion they've shown through the ages, to return us to the harmonious, partnership societies that existed in early times before the marauders, before patriarchy.

Now we have the tools to recover our worth. Now we have DNA, social media, and a variety of supportive groups popping up worldwide.

It's about the freedom to be all that is woman.

A BIRD'S EYE VIEW

Yes, I have lived long and experienced much. A brief world-view from 1932 would require volumes. So would a litany of all the meaningful events of my life.

That was never my purpose. My intent in writing this book was to set the story straight about Foods and Nutrition, my profession, to bring back curiosity, understanding, and respect. The circus of current and conflicting misinformation has people confused, afraid to eat. That hurts my heart. What hurts worse is the downhill slide of basic health and happiness.

As I wrote and revised, insights happened, increasing perspective. A pattern took shape. Here's what I saw:

A strong correlation exists between: 1) the decreasing physical and mental health in our society, and 2) the increase in the consumption of chemical/ pesticide-laden foods and man-made "foods" (about which we have little knowledge).

In general, food quality has been diminishing since the natural soil was "enhanced" with chemical fertilizers early in the century and pesticides were then used to save the weakened plants. Conventional food now lacks many nutrients and doesn't even taste the same anymore.

How is it that this has no voice?

Well, let's look at who's in charge. Right, BIG FOOD. Patriarchs. Not mothers, not caretakers, not those entrusted with the health and well-being of the human race.

Clearly, such a conversation would risk a financial crisis in Big Food and related industries that depend on our being needy and unhealthy. To increase income, business interests must increase consumption and disavow responsibility for the resulting ill health of trusting consumers. To support that, silence and dishonesty prevail.

Recently, in a bolt of insight, it all came together: the BIG picture.

Industry tactics include keeping customers ignorant and confused with cold, calculated, self-serving deceit <u>in the same way that patriarchy has controlled women for thousands of years.</u>

By studying woman's history, I see that the influence of our patriarchal culture had more to do with my life, every woman's life, than I had ever noticed just bobbing along, living life one day at a time, doing my best, deflecting degradation, moving on.

It's not just women who have suffered from patriarchy. Everyone has suffered. Every man, woman, and child. Every animal. Every living thing.

A deep look from past to future shows that we are on a path to end the single-minded stranglehold of money- and power-motivated patriarchy. History suggests that now is a perfect time to escalate our rebellion—right now, during these times of intense political and social upheaval.

We must stand up for sustainable agriculture, healthy food, and truthful information. Stand up for women's rights, for everyone's right to be respected as a human being. For honesty and integrity on all fronts.

Yes, let's take a bird's eye view into a meaningful future, a time when we care for our planet, our food, and one another together in a partnership society. We've been there before, five to seven thousand years ago, before patriarchy. It's time to come home again.

EPILOGUE

❧ FOOD ❧

For thousands of years, food came from the earth.
People honored the planet. They survived.
Food is now created for profit by greed. It is destroying the planet.
People are not healthy.
Visionaries are turning back to nature.
Some will survive.

❧ NUTRITION ❧

Most people now hold a reductionist view.
It's complicated, causes confusion, and inspires fraud.
Holistic views are returning.
Fraud and trickery are being challenged.

❧ WOMEN'S RIGHTS ❧

Ignorance reigns.
The long history of gender patterns will not die quickly.
Women will make inroads to mollify abuse.
The young will effect a paradigm shift.
Partnership economics of a caregiving society will return.

❧ SHIFTING LEADERSHIP ❧

Thought Leaders (the 1%) are replacing spin doctors.
Fear-mongering and deliberate acts to confuse us continue to enslave.
Most people remain subservient owing to their ignorance and blind trust.
Thought Leaders will self-destruct.

❦ KNOWLEDGE ❦

Information is expanding exponentially.
Right or wrong, it is data to be consumed.
Knowledge requires cultivation by unbiased minds.
It factors in that which we do not know.

❦ WHAT NOW? ❦

History is nipping at our heels.
We're at a tipping point.
We can lurch forward or fallback.
It's up to us.

APPENDICES

TRUSTWORTHY INFORMATION

Consumers face the near-impossible task of sifting through the noise for reliable and accurate information about food and nutrition. Find accurate facts in these appendices, simple, basic information. No fluff. No crap.

APPENDIX 1

Food Words in a Nutshell

Clarifying Definitions

✑ FOOD ✑

Conventional Definition
Any nourishing substance that is eaten, drunk, or otherwise taken into the body to sustain life, provide energy, promote growth, etc.

FDA Definition
(1) Articles used for food or drink for man or other animals.
(2) Chewing gum.
(3) Articles used for components of any such article.

Traditional
According to the customs or usual practices associated with a particular society, place, or set of circumstances.
According to a person's habitual practice.

Organic
The term "organic" has an established legal definition in many countries, including the United States, as well as an agreed-upon international standard. Therefore, all natural and organic products are not the same. In some countries, the term "natural" is defined and enforced. In others, it is not.

Natural
"Natural foods" and "all natural foods" are widely used terms in food labeling and marketing with a variety of definitions, most of which are vague. The term is assumed to imply foods that are minimally processed and do not contain manufactured ingredients, but that may or may not be the case.

Real Food
Whole foods that are unrefined and unprocessed and do not contain added ingredients.

Processed Food

Food transformed from raw ingredients into food, or created by modifying the ingredients or forms of existing food products. Food processing typically takes clean, harvested crops or butchered animal products and uses them to produce attractive, marketable, and often long shelf-life food products.

Frankenfoods

Genetically modified foods.

∽ NUTRIENTS ∽

Essential Nutrients

These are nutrients the body needs for health, growth, maintenance, etc., but cannot make, or cannot make in sufficient quantities. We must get these nutrients from the foods we eat, by fortifying food products, and in some cases, through dietary supplements.

Water

Indispensable and abundant, water forms the major part of almost every body tissue. Water is the environment in which nearly all the body's activities are conducted, such as maintaining our temperature, electrolyte balance, cellular fluid, transporting nutrients from here to there, as a lubricant and shock absorber.

Water comes from drinking it, from food and from beverages. It happens when the hydrogen from metabolism combines with oxygen in the air we breathe to form water. Too little water causes dehydration; too much causes water intoxication.

Protein

Protein is a vital structural and working material of all cells, performing function and regulation of the body's tissues and organs. Proteins are made up of smaller units called amino acids, which are attached to one another in long chains. The body continuously uses proteins. To rebuild protein, the body needs dietary protein.

Natural protein can be found in animal sources like meat and dairy products, or plant sources like beans, nuts, and seeds. Favorite concentrated sources are whey, a by-product of the cheese industry, and soy protein isolate, of questionable safety.

Know that the body cannot store proteins or amino acids. Excess protein will be broken down in your liver, the nitrogen portion excreted, and the rest stored as carbohydrate and fat.

Carbohydrates

Foods high in carbohydrates are an essential part of a healthy diet. Carbohydrates provide the body with glucose, which is converted to energy used to support bodily functions and physical activity. Quality matters; some types of carbohydrate-rich foods are better than others.

The healthiest sources of carbohydrates are from unprocessed or minimally processed whole grains, vegetables, fruits, and beans. They promote good health by delivering vitamins, minerals, fiber, and a host of important phytonutrients.

Unhealthier sources of carbohydrates include sodas, white bread, pastries, other highly processed or refined foods, and sugar in its many forms. These items contain easily digested carbohydrates that may contribute to weight gain, interfere with weight loss, and promote diabetes and heart disease. (There are over 300 names for added sugar, a total that keeps growing. See Appendix 4.)

Fibers are a class of compounds related to the carbohydrates but that do not yield energy. Their function is to keep food moving through the digestive system. Fibers keep the digestive tract clean, the digestive muscles healthy, and carry harmful substances out of the body.

Fat

The word "fat" is commonly used to include all lipids. Lipids include triglycerides (fats and oils), phospholipids (e.g., lecithin), and sterols (e.g., cholesterol).

Fats from animal and vegetable sources provide a concentrated source of energy. They also provide the building blocks for cell membrane and a variety of hormones and hormone-like substances.

Triglycerides carry the four fat-soluble vitamins, A, D, E, and K, together with many of the compounds that give foods their flavor, aroma, tenderness, and palatability.

Fat as part of a meal slows down absorption so we can go longer without feeling hungry.

Total Fat – Amount of fat in a single serving of food.

Saturated Fat – Usually solid at room temperature. They are found in animal products such as meat and milk, as well as in coconut and palm oil. Saturated fat is often used in foods to prevent rancidity and off flavors.

Polyunsaturated Fat – Found in nuts, fish, and edible oils. They provide essential fatty acids such as omega-3s and omega-6s.

Trans Fat – They are created when liquid fats such as vegetable oil are hydrogenated into more solid fats, such as margarine and shortening. This artificial fat is now considered to be unhealthy.

Vitamins

Vitamins serve as catalysts (helpers) making possible the processes by which the other nutrients are digested, absorbed, metabolized, and excreted. Natural vitamins are fragile and can be destroyed by processing, heat, light and chemical agents. Thirteen vitamins are essential for life, each with its own unique role to play.

Minerals

Nutritional minerals are tiny, pure inorganic elements in simple chemical forms, either alone or in combination with other nutrients. They are not metabolized, per se, but do influence metabolism.

These are the minerals essential for life:
calcium, chromium, copper, fluoride, iodine, iron, magnesium, manganese, molybdenum, phosphorus, potassium, selenium, sodium, and zinc.

Toxic minerals, such as lead, disrupt body functions.

∽ SUPPLEMENTS ∽

Dietary supplementation is intended to provide food nutrients that may be insufficient in one's diet due to poor growing conditions, poor diet, or illness. They are not meant to prevent or treat any disease and in some circumstances are dangerous.

Non-dietary supplements, such as body-building or herbal supplements, should only be taken upon recommendation of a professional health-care provider.

✑ PROCESSING TERMS ✑

Additives

Any substance that is reasonably expected to become a component of food is a food additive that is subject to premarket approval by FDA. There are exceptions: substances generally recognized as safe (GRAS) or that meet other exclusions from the food additive definition of the Federal Food, Drug, and Cosmetic Act (FFDCA).

Flavor Enhancers

Pure monosodium glutamate (MSG) and its cousins disodium inosinate and disodium guanylate, are salts of glutamic acid. They impart a unique taste sensation, called umami. They intensify the meaty, savory flavor of such foods like stews and meat-based soups. They cause similar side effects.

When MSG is contained as an ingredient in other food additives, it doesn't need to be labeled. People who experience MSG's side effects can learn to identify the hidden sources of MSG. (See Appendix 4.)

Flavorings – Natural vs. Artificial

Natural flavors must be derived from plant or animal material. Artificial flavors are synthesized in the lab. The chemicals in these two may be exactly the same: meaning, the chemical structures of the individual molecules may be indistinguishable using technology as we know it. Your body may be able to tell the difference.

Cost matters: a natural flavor almost always costs more than an artificial flavor. Still, food makers are often willing to pay because they know that some consumers prefer "natural" flavors. Often, natural and artificial flavors are mixed, as natural flavors not only cost more but also are not always consistently available.

Colors

Color additives are available for use in food as either "dyes" or "lakes." They are either artificial or natural. Artificial colors are highly regulated, whereas, dyes from natural foods are not.

Preservatives

Preservation is generally meant to avoid spoilage, maintain appearance, and increase usage time.

Traditional preservation includes pickling, boiling, freezing, refrigerating, dehydrating, smoking, and/or adding salt, sugar or vinegar.

Commercially, natural or chemical food preservatives are used.

Chemicals used as preservatives may be benzoates, nitrites, sulfites, sorbates, antioxidants like vitamin C, butylated hydroxytoluene (BHA), or bacterial growth inhibitors such as chelating agents or antimicrobial agents.

Added Sugars

Added sugars are sugars and syrups added to foods or beverages when they are processed or prepared. This does not include naturally occurring sugars such as those in milk and fruits.

Reading the ingredient label on processed foods can help to identify added sugars. Names for added sugars on food labels include:

anhydrous dextrose
brown sugar
confectioner's powdered sugar
corn syrup
corn syrup solids
dextrose
fructose
high fructose corn syrup (HFCS)
honey
invert sugar
lactose
malt syrup
maltose
maple syrup
molasses
nectars
  (e.g., peach nectar, pear nectar)

pancake syrup
raw sugar
sucrose
sugar
white granulated sugar

Other names are used for added sugars, but aren't recognized by the FDA as an ingredient name. These include:
  cane juice
  evaporated corn sweetener
  crystal dextrose
  glucose
  liquid fructose
  sugar cane juice
  fruit nectar

There are over 350 names for sugar, a total that keeps growing. (See Appendix 4.)

Dough Conditioners
Dough conditioners shorten dough rising times, increase shelf-life, and make the dough easier for machinery to process.

Anti-foaming agents
This additive is used to prevent the formation of foam or is added to break down a foam already formed. Commonly used agents include insoluble oils, polydimethylsiloxanes and other silicones, certain alcohols, stearates, and glycols.

Anticaking Agents
Anticaking Agent is the food additive that prevents agglomeration in particular solids, permitting a free-flowing condition. Anticaking agents consist of such substances as starch, magnesium carbonate, and silica, and are added to fine-particle solids, such as food products like table salt, flours, coffee, and sugar.

Antioxidants
A substance like vitamin C that inhibits oxidation, especially one used to counteract the deterioration of stored food products.

Color Retention Agents
These are food additives that prevent the color from changing. Many of them work by absorbing or binding to oxygen before it can damage food (antioxidants). For example, ascorbic acid (vitamin C) is often added to brightly colored fruits, such as peaches, during canning.

Emulsifiers
These substances stabilize the emulsions in particular food additives that are used to stabilize processed foods.

Flour Treatment Agents
Also called improving agents, bread improvers, dough conditioners, and dough improvers, these agents are food additives combined with flour to improve baking functionality. Flour treatment agents are used to increase the speed of dough rising and to improve the strength and workability of the dough.

Food Acids
Food acids are added to make flavors "sharper" and to act as preservatives and antioxidants. Acidity regulators are used to control the acidity and alkalinity of foods. Typical food acids are vinegar, tartaric acid, citric acid, malic acid, fumaric acid, and lactic acid.

Glazing Agents

Glazing agents produce a protective coating and impart a polish/sheen on the surface of food such as confectionery or citrus fruit or even baked goods.

Humectants

When used as a food additive, a humectant has the effect of keeping the foodstuff moist.

Typical humectants are honey and glucose syrup, both used for their water absorption and sweet flavors.

Propellants

Propellants help expel the food from its container. They are sealed under pressure in an aerosol food container. Standard propellants are carbon dioxide, nitrogen, nitrous oxide, butane, isobutane, propane, and octafluorocyclobutane

Stabilizers

Stabilizers smooth the texture of the food and give it body. They give a uniform nature to the product and hold the flavoring compounds in the dispersion.

Thickeners and Vegetable Gums

Substances that are added to food preparations for increasing their viscosity without changing other properties like the taste. Commonly used thickening agents are pectin, lignin, algin, gums, and agar-agar.

APPENDIX 2

The ABCs of Nutrition
Size, Metabolism, and Balance

Understanding the concepts of size, metabolism, and balance will bring clarity to the many issues around food and nutrition and the body.

cs **A** cs

SIZE

We are dealing with itty-bitty sub-microscopic particles of matter when we talk food. Not bagels, eggs, carrots, strawberries. Molecules. There are 1,760,000,000,000,000,000,000 molecules of sucrose in one teaspoon of sugar. 1.76×10^{21}. (Sucrose is made of two molecules of glucose.)

To picture that number, go to the internet and Google *Powers of Ten* video 1977. Take the slider in to 5.36 minutes, let the video engage, and watch as it rolls along to 6.46 minutes. Stop. That is the size of a molecule, albeit a white cell. That's close enough.

Molecules are three-dimensional structures composed of atoms. They have weight, mass, polarity, spin, and magnetism. They move continuously at high speed. They communicate. They attract one another, and link and unlink like puzzle pieces. They work together in symphony to get things done. That's called synergism.

An infinite number of food molecules are in a meal. We humans have only a vague idea of how they are metabolized and function. We can't measure things that small at that speed, much less with any understanding.

Human beings do not have the tools nor the mental capacity to know and understand such complicated matters, nor to grasp what we don't know. (See Appendix 7 - <u>Articles</u> - "How Little We Know,")

⍦ B ⍦

METABOLISM

Metabolism is a word we hear often, but may not understand. Because it is complex. It embraces the whole range of biochemical processes that occur within a living organism.

Two complementary systems are involved: catabolism and anabolism. Catabolism involves the breakdown of bodily tissues. Like when you exercise, breathe, or your heart beats. Anabolism involves the replacement of these tissues when you eat food.

Let's get a sense of metabolism by thinking first about food. Humans eat plants and the animals that have eaten the plants. Plants grow in soil, the loose top layer of the Earth's surface. It consists of rock and mineral particles mixed with decayed organic matter (humus). Soil is capable of retaining water, providing nutrients for plants, and supporting a broad range of biotic communities. Soil is a complex world of billions of organisms whose interactions create a nurturing environment for plants.

Plants grow by their internal process of photosynthesis using the sun's energy. They make simple carbohydrates like glucose and transform them into macronutrients like proteins and lipids.

This reaction **only** proceeds with an input of **solar** energy, called 'life force.'

Dictionary.com defines life force as the condition that distinguishes *organisms* from inorganic objects and dead organisms, being manifested by growth through metabolism, reproduction, and the power of adaptation to environment through changes originating internally.

Organisms get their energy from the sun via photosynthesis. We get our energy by eating the plants and animals that eat those plants. Life force is solar energy. The energy content of all natural food molecules can be traced back to the sun.

Being natural organisms ourselves, we fare better when getting our energy from nature.

Look at what has happened to human health—physically and mentally—since replacing natural food with fake food. Industrial/factory foods are awash with modified ingredients, food particles, plastic and other inorganic particles, pesticides, mysterious compounds, byproducts of pharmaceuticals, and chemicals that our bodies do not seem to recognize.

Engineered foods and manufactured foods are dead food. They have no life force (e.g., Doritos, Froot Loops, margarine, soy milk, whey). Processed foods have been compromised depending on the level of processing (e.g., lightly processed, such as fresh-squeezed orange juice, not so bad vs. ultra-processed milk, destroying all living components and denaturing the protein).

Life force was a common term until recently; now you never hear it or even think about it. WHY? Simple. Not good for the processed food business.

The ability of fake foods to engage in the metabolic processes of humans has never been studied. At the very least, we know that the life force is missing.

When people eat dead food, manufactured food, and compromised food, their bodies will crave the sun's energy via plants, directly and indirectly. They will keep eating, eating, eating—never satisfied, always hungry, often ingesting chemicals that mimic the sensation of life force, such as sugar and cocaine.

With an understanding of metabolism, consumers can make better food choices.

ᄵ C ᄵ

BALANCE

When people talk about balanced nutrition or a balanced diet, they are referring to the foods that a person's metabolism needs to meet the demands of their body at a particular time. A balanced diet for a toddler differs from a balanced diet for a football player. When a person is ill, their normal balance may need to be modified for a few days.

Of course, there are foundation food elements needed by all people. We all need carbohydrates, proteins, fats, vitamins, minerals, fiber, etc. The government's *Dietary Guidelines for Americans* over the years were intended to help us understand the amounts of each of the basic foods that had been shown to keep us healthy.

These guidelines have been influenced by competition within the food industry during the past few decades. This has impacted consumer's trust and empowered the diet and supplement industries. They, too, are profit motivated. To entice consumers, the promotion of these products continues to focus on health and wellness benefits that may not exist.

Worse, nearly all popular diets are not in balance. Understand that the body seeks balance: homeostasis. It will dump nutrients that are in excess. If your diet has too little of a necessary nutrient, your body will try to compensate or will malfunction slowly over time.

Traditional diets have at least stood the test of time. Hundreds and thousands of years. Traditional diets exhibit a balance of available natural foods learned over time.

No industrially manufactured foods have stood the test of time. Or any test. All of us are the test animals.

APPENDIX 3

Snake-Oil Salesmen

*Experts, Orchestrating Consumption, Slick and
Slippery Words and Phrases, Popular Science*

✧ EXPERTS ✧

One of the joys of growing old is realizing how little I know. How little anyone knows about nutrition.

To "know" something is to have learned a great deal from teachers, schools, books, and seminars.

Every field has its foundation. The ABCs are literally necessary to read or write. 2 + 2 is still 4. H_2O is still water. Even though food and nutrition are vast and complex subjects, they too rest on foundations.

In addition to an academic foundation, having personal experience provides a broader, deeper understanding. While one can know about carrots from books, that knowledge is enhanced by growing, cooking, and eating carrots.

Yet even when experts are brilliant and have done due-diligence, they can only pass on their understanding of the subject. Other brilliant experts may have different views on the same topic.

Even an expert can never know everything there is to know. Because there is no such thing. No absolute, proof positive, true answer.

Just ideas.

Everything changes every microsecond. Humans analyze information then compute possibilities and probabilities. But by the time they make a pronouncement, it's already out of date. There are billions of people on the planet. They, too, have ideas.

What can we do if there are no true answers? We do the next-best thing. We study, ask experts, get opinions, and come up with a "belief." A belief is what a person decides he/she will accept as fact or truth. Belief becomes a useful tool for them.

When a person shares information, by whatever means, they are actually sharing their ideas and beliefs about the subject.

Beliefs aren't forever. All beliefs are vulnerable to change, for as our view of reality changes, so do our beliefs.

My long-held definition of an expert as having "Knowledge plus Experience" is not sufficient anymore. Now I believe that an expert must have Knowledge, Experience, and a keen awareness that they do not know what they do not know. That's Wisdom.

Wise experts walk their talk and have nothing to sell.

ഽ ORCHESTRATING CONSUMPTION ഽ

Industry must sell product to make a profit; customers must buy. Customers are a picky bunch. They want new and exciting products that promise great taste, low price, and health benefits. And so, fads are created periodically to keep interest high and the dollars rolling in.

The movement of factory food onto a customer's plate is planned, coordinated, and choreographed by food and beverage companies, the grocery stores and the media. How does this manifest? It's a cooperative multi-industry strategy.

First, "spin doctors" are hired. Their job is to mold public opinion. They create a need and then supply the solution. They start by funding "scientific" studies to support the plan, engaging "experts," hiring lobbyists, wooing political advocates, and staffing government policing agencies. Whatever it takes.

After the spin doctors set the stage, the dance begins. Grocery stores are stocked, advertising gets underway with media blitzes, success stories, doctor recommendations, celebrity endorsements, books and blogs, new diets, recipes, cookbooks, and TV shows.

The vocabulary of marketing and advertising uses "alternate" words and phrases to attract the customer's interest, deceive them with false facts, and even frighten them into buying.

An alert shopper is wary of:

✓ <u>Reports and stories marked "Sponsored."</u>
These are links to paid advertising.

✓ <u>All research, studies, etc., that were paid for by any company or person with a vested interest in the results.</u>
This is most of what you see on the web. Check the source.

✓ <u>Popular Science.</u>
Everything that isn't real science.
Mostly entertainment and advertising.
Real science doesn't say, prove, suggest, show. It's just numbers. (For further explanation, see below.)

✍ SLICK AND SLIPPERY WORDS ✍

And Phrases Intended to Trick You

Here's a list. New ones come up all the time.

- Science says, Everybody knows, Proof positive, etc.
- May, might, could, promises, shows promise, shocking, mind-blowing, revelation, changes lives, stunning, jaw-dropping, insane, cracks reality wide-open, you should, you shouldn't, you must, you have to, sold out in 2 days, exploded on the internet, took social media by storm, etc.
- "Approved" or "Recommended" by experts, doctors, chiropractors, nutritionists, dieticians, celebrities, talk-show hosts, exercise instructors, etc. These are too vague. No name.
- "Sponsored" articles. That's another word for "advertisement." On the internet, "Sponsored" should appear above the title of the news piece, but often is disguised as real news.
- Articles that entice you then require you to advance page-by-page. Each of those pages has cookies to get your information or preferences.

- Words that suggest a relationship: link, correlate, yoke. Like, "Chewing gum has been linked to cancer." (Links, etc. do NOT cause effects.)

- Percentages. Example: "50% of all the women tested showed positive results." (What if only two women were tested?) (See *How to Lie with Statistics in* Appendix 7.)

- Confusing language. It's probably intended double-talk or just poor reporting.

- "Research" or claims that can't be tested. Example: "You will look ten years younger when you use Beauty's Secret on a daily basis."

- Claims that promise you a longer, healthier, or happier life. There's no way to know that.

- Vague, general words, like *protein*: What kind of protein? Animal protein or vegetable protein or laboratory-made protein? (There are 10s of thousands of proteins.) Or *milk*: Which milk? Raw milk, processed milk, canned milk, dry milk, cow milk, goat milk, camel milk?

- Hypothesis. First, there is theory or an idea, and then a hypothesis, which is a reasonable guess of how a theory could be examined/tested. Neither theory nor a hypothesis is a fact, or even a promise of a fact.

- Recognize meaningless advertising words like Natural, Fresh, Wholesome, Pure, Trusted, Healthy.

- Ignore reports/reporters who don't know that the word "data" is the plural of "datum." Would you trust the skills of an English teacher who would say, "The children is at lunch."?

○ POPULAR SCIENCE ○

Basic science, "Real Science," deals with numbers and probabilities. In essence, it is a game of chance. It is specific and is designed to compare similar things like apples and oranges. The "things" must be measurable, not like love or ideas. Well-designed scientific studies have strict guidelines: no bias, sufficient participants, no variables. (Essence of Science, p 60 – 61)

The results are reported in numbers and are analyzed with statistics. There is always a margin of error when dealing with biological issues, called "biological variability," it can be as high as 10 percent.

The *meaning* of the resulting numbers is interpreted/determined by human beings. People have bias and prejudices, especially if they have a vested interest in the outcome.

"Real science" is as good as it gets, however. The next level down is an "epidemiological study." Patterns of large numbers of differing groups are compared, and conclusions are drawn.

Science has limitations. It cannot adequately address most of the questions that people want answered. So people make up answers. And believe them because they want to.

This is called "Popular Science," a cancer that preys on people's lack of basic scientific knowledge and hunger for answers to real questions and solutions to real problems. The prostitution of science is cruel and stupid. Arrogance and ignorance run amuck. Doomed for lack of respect. It harms everyone.

APPENDIX 4

Hidden Sources of Sugar, Hidden Sources of MSG, and Over 600 Diets

Links

⁓ Hidden Sources of Sugar ⁓

For the past six years, Jeremy Goodwin has counted the many names of sugar and reported them on his Facebook page. His latest number in 2016 was 340 names.

https://www.facebook.com/notes/single-mans-kitchen/all-the-249-names-of-sugar-so-far-project/10150839799498198

⁓ Hidden Sources of MSG ⁓

The website *Truth in Labeling* lists names of ingredients that contain processed free glutamic acid (MSG.) Last updated March 2014.

http://www.truthinlabeling.org/hiddensources.html

⁓ List of Over 600 Diets ⁓

Way over-the top, this website clearly shows the insanity of dieting. "Our complete list of over 600 nutritionist-reviewed diets arranged in alphabetical order. Choose the diet plan that best fits your goals and lifestyle."

https://www.everydiet.org/diet

APPENDIX 5

What Do I Eat?

I'm "old-school," living well all my life on the traditional foods of my family for generations. My diet is basic traditional Caucasian, hailing from northern Europe.

I cook a lightweight Omnivore's menu with some meat, usually pork, potatoes, fresh seasonal vegetables, and fruit. I make bone broth-based soups and stews with seasonal vegetables, and sometimes beans. I eat plenty of raw butter, raw milk, yogurt, and cheese. An egg a day. Rarely bread or bakery products. Sometimes pasta, oats or rice. Drink coffee and tea in moderation.

I rarely use pharmaceuticals. I do use these supplements: cod-liver oil because I always have, desiccated liver caps now and then because I don't like liver, glucosamine chondroitin for my joints, and CBD sublingual drops to maintain full body homeostasis. Do they work? I don't know. I just trust the literature, and I feel good.

I take about half the recommended dosage of these supplements since I weigh a lot less than the average person.

My diet may not work for you if you are lactose intolerant. Not being able to drink milk may be due to a sensitivity/allergic response or to lactose intolerance. With raw milk, however, the lactose can be eliminated by letting the fresh milk "rest" for two days at room temperature. Lactose is a sugar; the bacteria lactase will eat it all up as the milk rests. This won't work with pasteurized milk since the pasteurization process kills the bacteria. If you let your raw milk rest and still have symptoms, the problem is likely a sensitivity or allergy to the protein.

I've not been motivated to try other diets because I've always been healthy and energetic, though I did try vegetarianism for a while. Advertising's bright lights, the dazzle of "bigger, better, and more," the ravings and rantings of self-appointed experts, and the allure of industrial goodies have gone over my head, in one ear and out the other, allowing me to enjoy a simple life and a healthy body.

I ignore the threats and overflowing misinformation of today's popular science and righteous gurus. I eat lots of raw butter and saturated fats. They add flavor to cooking and give 'body' to my meals. They support satiety, so I am rarely hungry. I love the taste and feel of creamy raw milk; it's especially soothing at night when I'm restless.

My annual physical in July 2017, age 84, put me at 5'1" tall, 111 pounds, blood pressure 100/60, heart rate 70, and cholesterol 170. The remaining stats are normal. They haven't changed since I started getting physicals at 65. My treadmill test two years ago was normal; my carotid arteries are clear. My hair and nails are healthy.

With marriage, I modified our family meals to incorporate my husbands' traditions, which then were passed on to the kids, and are now part of their heritage. (That's an example of epigenetics.) I've modified the food I eat during times of life demands, such as pregnancy, work schedules, the desire of others, and growing old.

I indulge in comfort foods now and then, like chocolate, Christmas cookies, pumpkin chiffon pie with gingersnap crust, and SPAM.

I avoid the following:

- MSG – Makes my fingers tingle and skin itch. (See Appendix 4 for hidden sources.)

- Table salt – No nutrition; just sodium and chloride. I use unprocessed salt that contains 80+ minerals.

- Sugar – It's not food, has no nutritive value, and it's addictive. (See Appendix 1: Added Sugars and Appendix 4: Sugar's 340+ other names.)

- Seed and nut oils except for olive oil. Getting the oil out of seeds and nuts involves a harsh extraction process that includes bleaching, deodorizing, and the toxic solvent hexane. The nutrient composition of the oils is imbalanced.

- Soy – Years after the Nigeria project ended, I learned that soy is loaded with anti-nutrients. No wonder the babies cried. Soy is significant in our food supply because it is a government-subsidized crop, so there is lots of it, and it's cheap. It is genetically modified like corn. And no, soy has not been eaten in the Orient for ages. Soy was used there as fertilizer, not food.

- Nut or bean "milk" – Highly processed, not much nutrition, primarily water, a bit of thickener, and artificial flavors.

* * *

Around 2010, a friend from the magnetic bed business emailed me. "I just went to a nutrition conference, and guess what? All those people there eat the same way you do." She gave me their website, and sure enough, it's true. It's the Weston A. Price Foundation, a non-profit organization promoting traditional foods and nutrition. What a joy to find like-minded folks. I joined, of course. I have found them to be serious scientists, dedicated to enhancing people's lives through natural nutrition.

In 2013, they held a regional convention in Portland, Oregon, not too far from Vegas. I went, basking in the moment, getting to know people, listening to talks given by authors whose books I had read, feeling as though I'd found lost family.

The Weston A. Price Foundation offers an abundance of up-to-date information and solutions. (See Appendix 7.)

APPENDIX 6

Recipe for Wellness

That magical state of feeling good nearly all the time,
rarely getting sick, and being able to handle life's trials with relative ease

- Eat consciously . . . three small, light, and healthy meals: a balance of fresh, natural, colorful, wholesome foods, grown locally when possible.

- Eat as the generations of your family have eaten. It's in your DNA, and it serves you well.

- Cook . . . so you'll know what you are eating. It's not hard to learn how.

- Learn about foods and nutrition from knowledgeable sources. Ask doctors doctor questions; ask nutritionists nutrition questions. Trust only experts in their field.

- Drink water . . . Enough, but not too much.

- Exercise rigorously five or six days a week: aerobics, strength, yoga/stretch. Also, be active: shop, garden, cook, clean, walk, etc. Rest one day a week.

- Get enough sleep.

- Breathe deeply. Sing (or hum). Laugh often.

- Be open to alternative modalities: vibration, magnets, sound, light, essential oils, acupuncture, and homeopathic and natural remedies.

- Take in nothing toxic. Do nothing toxic. Eliminate toxic people from your life.

- Socialize. Call family often. Nourish friendships.

- Read for knowledge. Read for fun. Do new stuff.

- Live in possibilities.

- Do good deeds.

- Whine less. Be grateful often.

- Bring art, music, flowers, and friends into your home.

APPENDIX 7

Reliable Resources

Those of us who are committed to having good health need to have truthful and accurate resources to guide our choices. These resources will identify a hand-full of basic, readable books and online sources to help you make educated and practical choices.

- It's not a listing of all the resources I've read/viewed.

- Nor all the good books and online offerings available.

- No books or sites that promote people's ideas or studies, interesting or possible as they may be.

- No books that promote products for sale.

- Popularity is irrelevant.

- Listed by year of publication.

❧ BOOKS ❧

Food and Nutrition

Nourishing Traditions: The Cookbook that Challenges Politically Correct Nutrition and the Diet Dictocrats - Sally Fallon with Mary G. Enig, 2001, NewTrends Publishing.

With respect for traditional diets coupled with the sound science of today, the authors educate and teach us how to prepare healthy food.

Healthy 4 Life: Dietary Guidelines from the Weston A. Price Foundation for Cooking and Eating Healthy, Delicious, Traditional Whole Foods - Available in paperback or pdf from the Weston A. Price Foundation.

These guidelines provide foods that are satisfying, delicious to eat, and healthy for you with recipes. Easy to follow.

Appetite for Profit: How the Food Industry Undermines Our Health and How to Fight Back - Michelle Simon, 2006, Basic Books.

Hard-hitting health-policy attorney Michelle Simon takes on the industrial food industry. Six appendices provide guides to industry groups, spin doctoring, myths and realities, schools, your legal rights, and resources for change.

Real Food: What to Eat and Why - Nina Planck, 2006, Bloomsbury USA.

Hailing from the world of farmer's markets, with personal stories bolstered by sound research, Nina Planck tells it like it is.

Kitchen Literacy: How We Lost Knowledge of Where Food Comes From and Why We Need to Get It Back - Ann Vileisis, 2008, Island Press.

A thorough and well-researched history of food in America. Fascinating, and not that long ago.

Deep Nutrition: Why Your Genes Need Traditional Food - Catherine Shanahan, MD, Luke Shanahan MFA, 2009, Big Box Book, HI.

Here you will discover the commonality of food consumption worldwide. This "Human Diet" is instinctively familiar to all of us, yet has twists and turns.

Food Rules: An Eater's Manual - Michael Pollan, 2009, Penguin.

A delightful little 80-page guide on choosing, buying, and eating healthy food.

Folks, This Ain't Normal: A Farmer's Advice for Happier Hens, Healthier People, and a Better World - Joel Salatin, 2011, Hachette Book Group.

A clear declaration that we need to corral the industrialized food system and focus instead on local and sustainable food production.

Eat Drink Vote: An Illustrated Guide to Food Politics - Marion Nestle, 2013, Rodale Books.

Enjoy learning about the problems and the politics around food with cartoons and comics.

The Dorito Effect: The Surprising New Truth about Food and Flavor - Mark Schatzker, 2015, Simon and Schuster.

A much-appreciated peek into the creation of non-food-foods and other industrial goodies that we eat.

Trickery

How to Lie with Statistics - Darrell Huff, illustrated by Irving Geis, 1954, WW Norton & Company.

First published 60 years ago as a tongue-in-cheek parody of statistics. Marketers use it so they can trick you. Now you can find out how to read between the lines.

Selling Sickness: How the World's Biggest Pharmaceutical Companies Are Turning Us All Into Patients - Ray Moynihan & Alan Cassels, 2005, Nation Books.

This provocative book takes on Merck's dream of selling pharmaceuticals to everyone, whether they need them or not, and exposing the fear-mongering that has us all fooled.

Women's History

When God Was a Woman - Merlin Stone, 1976, A Harvest/HBJ Book, Harcourt Brace Jovanovich Publishers.

A well-documented history of the most ancient of religions, the religion of the Goddess, and the role this ancient worship played in Judeo-Christian attitudes toward women. Facts vs. myths. Finally, I get it.

The Chalice & The Blade: Our History, Our Future - Riane Eisler, 1988, Harper Row.

This book tells a similar, but different story of our cultural origins. It shows that warfare and the war of the sexes are neither divinely nor biologically ordained. It provides verification that a better future is possible.

Who Cooked the Last Supper: The Women's History of the World - Rosalind Miles 1988, Three Rivers Press.

A fascinating, frightful, imperative history of women's contributions to the history of the world, the history we never learned, one that celebrates our contributions.

The Secret History of Wonder Woman - Jill Lepore, 2015, Vintage Books.

Delightful and rich with illustrations. Wonder Woman's history reveals the culture of the Women's Movement since the 1900s.

∽ ARTICLES ∽

"How Little We Know: 99% of The Microbes in Our Own Bodies Are Still a Total Mystery to Science" (Science Alert)

> http://www.sciencealert.com/more-than-99-percent-of-the-microbes-inside-us-are-unknown-to-science

"The Zoo Beneath our Feet - We're only beginning to understand soil's hidden world." (The Washington Post)

> https://www.washingtonpost.com/lifestyle/home/the-zoo-beneath-our-feet-were-only-beginning-to-understand-soils-hidden-world/2017/08/08/f73e3950-7799-11e7-9eac-d56bd5568db8_story.html?utm_term=.1302878039f7

"Why do we believe blatant untruths?" (The New York Times)

> https://www.nytimes.com/2017/03/03/opinion/sunday/why-we-believe-obvious-untruths.html?mcubz=1

∽ VIDEOS ∽

The Future of Food

> Under 10 minutes long, this video is a must-see. It offers an in-depth investigation into the disturbing truth behind the unlabeled, patented, genetically engineered foods.
>
> https://www.youtube.com/watch?v=XKtJcoccU-c

Oldways

> A Taste of African Heritage Program
>
> Traditional Foods – Pathway to Healing Webinar
>
> https://www.youtube.com/watch?v=2aBKAF_qzKA&feature=youtu.be

∽ ONLINE RESOURCES & CONNECTIONS ∽

These are the ones I follow at the moment. I'm always looking for knowledge and insight.

Environmental Working Group (EWG)

A US non-profit environmental organization addressing toxins, agricultural subsidies, public lands, and corporate accountability; "The Dirty 12/Clean 15," and quality ratings for thousands of food products.

www.ewg.org

Organic Consumers Organization (OAC)

A non-profit advocacy group for organic agriculture

www.organicconsumers.org

The Weston A. Price Foundation (WAPF)

A source for accurate information on nutrition and health, always aiming to provide the scientific validation of traditional foodways.

www.westonaprice.org

Food Democracy Now

A grassroots community dedicated to building a sustainable food system that protects our natural environment, sustains farmers, and nourishes families.

www.fooddemocracynow.org

Civil Eats

A daily news source for critical thought about the American food system.

www.civileats.com

Food Watch

An independent, non-profit organization that exposes food-industry practices that are not in the interests of consumers.

www.foodwatch.org

Food Politics with Marion Nestle

Sign in to "Follow Marion" to get her daily blog. She keeps us up-to-date with insight.

www.foodpolitics.com

Savory Global Institute

Successful studies and research designed to reclaim soil worldwide.

www.savory.global/institute/

Equal Rights Advocates

A national civil rights organization dedicated to protecting and expanding economic and educational access.

noreen@equalrights.org

The Women's' March

Building a strong, sustainable organization for change. Get connected.

www.facebook.com/womensmarchonwash/

Emily's List

"Everyday. Every election victory. We are helping to put women into office who have the power to put progressive change to work . . ."

www.emilyslist.org

APPENDIX 8

Documentation of My Research
During the years of 1960 – 1967

Kurtzman, C.H., D G. Snyder, and H.W. Nilson. "Cystine and Total Sulfhydryl Content of Unspoiled and Spoiled Shrimp." *Food Research*, 25, 2 (1960). Designed and conducted research; prepared manuscript.

Kurtzman, C.H., and D.G. Snyder. "The Picric Acid Turbidity Test – A Possible Practical Freshness Test for Iced Shrimp." *Food Technology*, 14, 7 (1960). Designed and conducted research; prepared manuscript.

Lee, C.F., L. Pepper, and C.H. Kurtzman. "Proximate Composition of Southern Oysters – Factors Affecting Variability." *Commercial Fisheries Review*, 22, 7 (1960). Conducted research; edited manuscript.

Kurtzman, C.H. "Now About that Nutrition Angle." *Seafood Merchandising*, XX, 9 (1960). Prepared Manuscript.

Kurtzman, C.H., and Donald G. Snyder. "A Rapid Freshness Test for Blue-Crab Meat and Observations on Spoilage Characteristics." *Commercial Fisheries Review*, 22, 11 (1960). Designed and supervised research; prepared manuscript.

Kurtzman, C.H. "Determination of the Protein Content and Nutritive Value of the Protein of Fish Flour." 1 – Screening Study of Available World Samples. 2 – The Effect of Some Processing Variables. M.S Thesis, The University of Maryland (1960). Designed and conducted research; prepared manuscript.

Kurtzman C.H., R.R. Kifer, and D.G. Snyder. "Rat-Feeding Studies to Determine Presence of Antimetabolites, Water-Soluble Vitamins, and Essential Minerals in Raw Menhaden as Compared with Raw Haddock and Beef." *Commercial Fisheries Review*, 24, 8, (1960). Designed research; both conducted some parts and supervised other parts of research; prepared manuscript.

Swain, R.L., and C.H. Kurtzman. "Food Research and Flavor Acceptance." *Candy Technology* (1960). Prepared Manuscript.

Kurtzman, C.H., D.G. Snyder, L.E. Ousterhout, F.T. Piskur, and P.F. Braucher. "Effect of Several Processing Variables on the Protein Content and Quality of Fish Flour." FAO, *Fish in Nutrition*, publ. 1962. Designed and conducted research; prepared manuscript (part of a chapter).

Kurtzman, C.H. "Fish Flour – A Food with a Future." *Seafood for Health and Nutrition*, Fisheries Marketing Bulletin, 62, 5A (1963). Prepared Manuscript.

Kurtzman, C.H. and L.B. Sjostrom. "The Flavor-Modifying Properties of Monosodium Inosinate." *Food Technology*, 18, 9 (1964). Designed research; conducted much of the research, supervised the rest; prepared manuscript.

Kurtzman, C.H., Preston Smith, Jr., and D.G. Snyder. "An Automated Method for the Determination of Cystine." *Analytical Biochemistry*, 12 2 (1965). Designed and conducted research; prepared manuscript.

Smith, Preston, Jr., C.H. Kurtzman, and M.E. Ambrose. "Automated Method for the Determination of Calcium in the Presence of Magnesium and Phosphate Ions using Dye Eriochrome Blue S.E." *Clinical Chemistry*, 12 7 (1966). Participated in research.

Kurtzman, C.H., and M.E. Ambrose. "An Accurate Method for Determination of the Cystine in Fish Meals and Fish Protein Concentrates." Report of the Bureau of Commercial Fisheries (1967). Participated in research.

Kurtzman, C.H. "The Effects of Flavor and Physical Properties of Additions of Fish Protein Concentrate on Yeast Bread and Dry Pea Soup." Designed and conducted research; prepared manuscript. I left that the Bureau of Commercial Fisheries and never found out where it was published. From my memory, however, I will tell you that neither the bread nor the soup tasted good. Fishy and gritty.

ABOUT THE AUTHOR

Caroline Anaya is educated in Foods and Nutrition with a BS from the University of Arizona and an MS from the University of Maryland. She helped develop human nutrition requirements with the US Department of Agriculture and quality standards for fishery products with the US Department of the Interior. She was a flavor technologist with Arthur D. Little, Inc. in Cambridge, Massachusetts, and a clinical nutritionist in rural Kansas. She has published a dozen scientific papers and articles. During midlife, Caroline worked a variety of jobs while raising three children. In later life, she was a fitness and yoga instructor while raising a grandson. Caroline is now actively retired.

www.TheBiteofHistory.com

Thank you for reading my book. Would you mind doing me a huge favor? Please write a customer review on Amazon for The Bite of History. Amazon promotes books that have 50 or more reviews. It doesn't matter if the reviews are good or bad. But they must be about the book itself. Review readers are looking for reasons to read or not read a book.

Thank you. Caroline

Made in the USA
Lexington, KY
01 December 2019

57921215R00122